Advance Praise for
It's Not About the Weight

Dr. Mendelsohn heartens with step by step advice on getting rational and active, heeding the feelings, and vaulting over the psychological barriers caused by a society dying to be thin. Anyone would benefit from her thoughts on being beautiful from the inside out. She wrestles the obsession with weight triumphantly to the ground!

—Gary Stromberg and Jane Merrill,
Authors of *Feeding the Fame: Celebrities Tell Their Real-Life Stories of Eating Disorders and Recovery*

Unique, practical, and remarkable insight into the struggle to overcome her ED, Dr. Susie examines the complexities of her illness, and offers sound and useful advice. To the point, easy to understand, inspiring, and helpful, the stories reveal the pain for the victim and struggle for interpersonal relationships. This is a must read for the family and loved ones of those suffering from ED. The words also provide practical psychological principles that encourage us to examine more closely examine this disorder and help guide its victims to a life of success rather than defeat.

—Jon E. Mendelsohn, MD, FACS
*Medical Director—Advanced Cosmetic Surgery and Laser Center
Cincinnati, OH*

Dr Mendelsohn's energy, compassion and expertise in the field of eating disorders recovery are remarkable. This heartfelt book is a valuable tool for patients, families and other professionals!

—Lisa West-Smith, PhD, LCSW, Psychotherapist, educator and author of *Body Stories: Research & Intimate Narratives on Women Transforming Body Image in Outdoor Adventure*

It's Not About the Weight

It's Not About the Weight

Attacking Eating Disorders from the Inside Out

Susan J. Mendelsohn, Psy.D.

iUniverse, Inc.
New York Lincoln Shanghai

It's Not About the Weight
Attacking Eating Disorders from the Inside Out

iUniverse books may be ordered through booksellers or by contacting:

iUniverse
2021 Pine Lake Road, Suite 100
Lincoln, NE 68512
www.iuniverse.com
1-800-Authors (1-800-288-4677)

The information, ideas, and suggestions in this book are not intended as a substitute for professional advice. Before following any suggestions contained in this book, you should consult your personal physician or mental health professional. Neither the author nor the publisher shall be liable or responsible for any loss or damage allegedly arising as a consequence of your use or application of any information or suggestions in this book.

ISBN-13: 978-0-595-41883-1 (pbk)
ISBN-13: 978-0-595-86231-3 (ebk)
ISBN-10: 0-595-41883-X (pbk)
ISBN-10: 0-595-86231-4 (ebk)

Printed in the United States of America

This book is dedicated to … all of the males, females, boys, girls, teenagers, moms, dads, boyfriends, girlfriends, brothers, sisters, aunts, uncles, friends, cousins, kids, grandparents, coaches, teachers, doctors, nurses, clergy, etc., whose lives have been touched by a loved one or someone they know who has suffered by the chains of ED.

I lived with ED, I hated ED, and I loved ED. He was my hero, he was my friend, and he was my enemy: He was there when no one else would listen to me. He saved me. He ruined me. He loved me. He destroyed me.

I won't let that happen to you …

The bottom line is this: I have an eating disorder. I'm happy now, I'm healthy, I look good and feel good—yes, I even feel good about how I look—but I did have, still have, and will always have an ED. That makes it especially easy for me to counsel others with EDs, and particularly hard for me as well. I know that there but for the grace of God go I, and every patient who ever sits across from me is a mirror for my own insecurities, shame, pride, ego, dread, hope, and fear.

—Dr. Susan Mendelsohn

Contents

Acknowledgments

There are many people who pave the way for future accomplishments. In all that I've done, in all that I've tried to do, even in the writing of this book, I consider myself the "tip of the spear." Many came before me and countless more will. For now I content myself with thanking those individuals that supported me along the way.

First and foremost I want to thank my family: Sally, Bobbie, Stan, Mark, Jon, Scott, Dan, Dave, Hannah, Benny, Cole, and Freddy. Some of these people you will read about in this book; others you will not. However, all have had a deep impact on my life, for better or for worse. We cannot change the past, nor can we predict the future, but we can live in the here and now. As an ED survivor, that is my most daunting challenge. My family has supported me in that challenge, most notably in the writing of this very personal and emotional book. I thank them all and wish for our continued healing as we all move together toward a brighter future.

To Fr. Martin Devereaux, Clinical Psychologist: He was my professor, supervisor, colleague, mentor, and friend. After being my professor in my first master's degree program, "Marty" gave me my start co-leading therapy groups with him at the church. He provided me with my first therapy office; he asked me to teach for him while he took his sabbatical from the university. Eventually, he became my supervisor for my clinical hours, and he was always my friend through thick and thin. He never had a judgmental bone in his body and was always there for me. He provided unconditional positive regard, listened with an open mind, and loved me for me. Thank you, Marty, for being my solace in my crazy, mixed-up world from the very beginning of my academic and professional journey.

To Dr. Mohammed Latif: Thank you for providing me the professional courtesy that I so needed when I was at my lowest point of my life. Thank you for your trust in my ability to prove myself and to succeed.

To Dr. Scott Fehr: Thank you for believing in me and for being the first person in the entire universe who ever really fully understood me. Thank you for being the first and only human being in my life who has ever validated *me* for *me*. Hey, a bit of advice: Don't ever apologize to me again for telling me that I'm not crazy! It was a breath of fresh air for a change! And thank you for gently forcing me to take the very necessary time off from work that every psychologist requires in this line of challenging work and for providing me the opportunity to express my true creative being from the inside out.

To Max Aubry, my personal kickboxing trainer. Not only do I crave my daily workouts, but you've given me back my zest for life! Your personal training has provided me with my mental, physical and psychological endurance that allows me to live my life to its fullest every single day!

To Rusty Fischer: Without Rusty I could never have completed this manuscript after pondering it for over six long years. By myself I could not find the right words to articulate what I needed to express about the seriousness of eating disorders. Rusty took on this project without knowing the challenges of ED or psychology itself. He persevered, learned, and sweated while I challenged him with the psychological terminology and the chaos that ED causes in the minds of his victims. And here we are with this extraordinary document! Thank you, Rusty, from the bottom of my heart, for your diligent work and for coaching me through this tedious process of writing my first true manuscript.

To all of my colleagues in Ohio and Kentucky who have made my career possible by working side-by-side with me to assist our patients in their recovery from an eating disorder:

- Brian Dowling, MD (Psychiatric Medicine)
- David Lim, MD (Internal Medicine)
- Petra Hackenberg-Bauer, MD (Adolescent Medicine)
- Laurie Mitan, MD (Adolescent Medicine)
- Corinne Lehmann, MD (Adolescent Medicine)
- Aimee Rusk, MD (Psychiatric Medicine)
- Nicole Hemmert, RD (Registered Dietician)

- Amy Bellamah-Daniels, RD (Registered Dietician)

- Ann Rooney, RD (Registered Dietician)

- Ann Marie Kemer, RD (Registered Dietician)

- Lisa West-Smith, PhD, LCSW (Doctor of Philosophy, Licensed Clinical Social Worker)

- Stacy Gregovich, Exercise Physiologist

- PJ Striet, Exercise Physiologist

And, finally, in loving memory of Uncle Fred, who pushed me to my limits all the while still loving me and reminding me that I had not only beauty but brains when I graduated college in 1985: I thank him for trusting me with his secrets … and for loving me even when I didn't love myself.

He taught me many life lessons—some healthy, some unhealthy, but all lessons that helped me to grow and become the professional that I am now. I have missed him every single day of my life since he passed away. I wish he could see me now and be proud of me, the way I have become proud of myself. I love you, Freddy, and always have!

Introduction

"What would have helped me? Maybe if I had been treated like a person, instead of an anorexic. People aren't anorexic or bulimic, they have it. It's sad being referred to as a disorder."

—Anonymous ED sufferer

American reporter Jill Carroll, a freelance writer on assignment in Iraq for the *Christian Science Monitor*, was kidnapped on January 7, 2006, by unidentified gunmen in western Baghdad. For the next three months, Jill wondered from day to day whether she would die a hostage. "It was like falling off a cliff for three months, waiting to hit the ground," the twenty-eight-year-old American reporter said after finally being released by her kidnappers in late March.

Three months without exercise had made her face round. Her captors had treated her well, she said, and she never dared to turn down their offers of meals or candy for fear of giving offense.

"I'm fat," was one of the first things she said upon her release.

"I'm fat."

Yes, she was thankful that her kidnappers hadn't killed her. Yes, she was grateful that they'd let her go, unharmed (except for those nagging extra pounds!). Yes, she was relieved that she'd finally be going home to America, her family, and (we assume) her exercise regimen. But still, as she faced those American values that say rescued hostages should look as glamorous and sexy as Kim Basinger at the end of the movie *Cellular,* she uttered the perfect two-word anti-climactic statement of a back-to-reality American girl at heart: "I'm fat."

And we wonder why, according to the National Eating Disorders Association, "In the United States, as many as ten million females and one million males are fighting a life and death battle with an eating disorder such as anorexia or bulimia. Approximately twenty-five million more are struggling with binge eating disorder …"

Few authors know the statistics as well as I do, as the official psychologist for eDiets.com. And few therapists know the horrors as well as I, as I myself have grappled with eating disorders, on and off, for over twenty years. While many who suffer from eating disorders, otherwise known as EDs, have penned touching memoirs and many more therapists have reacted with self-help books on the sensitive topic, to date there has yet to be a self-help memoir written by a doctor who herself has suffered with EDs. Nor has there been an ED book that spoke not just to the exposed ribs, weak tooth enamel, anemia, and signs of wasting that are so chronic to the physical aspects of the disease, but also to the emotional debate that rages inside, untouched by most traditional or over-the-counter methods of dealing with ED. Part and parcel of my inside-out therapy—and the cornerstone of my new book—is to treat the disease first and the symptoms second—the inside *before* the outside.

It's Not About the Weight: Attacking Eating Disorders from the Inside Out helps shatter the myths that surround eating disorders. These myths have worked to the disadvantage of an entire generation of individuals who have grown up thinking that if they merely "lose weight" or "look healthier" their problems are licked.

However, EDs are not about weight management. Fasting, starving oneself, bingeing, purging, weight gain, and weight loss are merely physical manifestations of an internal cause. They are the exterior façade of a crumbling, decaying, rotting emotional morass of pain and discontent caused by years of unresolved emotional issues. Gaining self-insight into one's body image is the first step in overcoming the inner turmoil affecting one's overall mental, physical, and psychological well-being.

As the official psychologist for eDiets.com, I answer questions about body image preoccupation or distortion all day long. As a therapist treating patients with full-blown eating disorders, I face life or death on a daily basis. This claim is far from hyperbole; according to ANRED (Anorexia and Related Eating Disorders, Inc.), "Without treatment, up to 20 percent of people with serious eating disorders die."

This semi-autobiographical book focuses on my story of growing up with and growing through the conundrum of body image distortions. I have also included real-life cases of my clinical practice in conjunction with the challenges of the members of eDiets.com with whom I have consulted since 1998. The self-help element is based on sound scientific research versus real life, homespun information. Rather than short vignettes, there is a continuous story of my growth as a complete process. This success story educates the reader to apply steps in overcoming the obstacles of weight and body image, how to manage weight during recovery triumphantly, how to maintain an overall satisfying existence, and how to finally *live* no matter what shape, size, or weight the reader is at any given moment.

Throughout each chapter, highlighted text gives actual psychological principles to assist the reader in identifying current theories related to specific eating disorders and weight challenges.

Just as I present an informal therapeutic environment, the book is also a friendly guide showing how to make changes rather then *telling* the audience to change. This narrative guides the audience to integrate these changes through practical application rather than theoretical learning. At the same time, the book, offers the reader the opportunity to learn about the concrete reasoning behind the steps necessary to follow successful recovery and an overall healthy and balanced lifestyle.

Letters to ED, to our bodies, to ourselves:

Dear ED,

There is no logical explanation for our relationship. I despise you with all the hate and loathing that I contain. You have stolen my friends, my family, my emotions, my health, and my life. You have murdered me. You made a promise and broke it. You lied to me. You convinced me that everything in the world was one way and I found that it wasn't that way at all. You led me down a path of deception and destruction and you crushed me. Then you abandoned me leaving me cold, alone, terrified, and lost.

While I hate you for all of this, you have been all that I have had. You've been my closest friend and companion. When we were close, I loved you. I thought we'd be together forever and I loved that thought. You picked me up when I was down; comforted me when I was hurting, and loved me when no one else did. I couldn't imagine life without you. I know that we are over. Our friendship has to end. For so long you seemed to complete me. Even my friends met you and didn't say anything. No words of comfort, warning, or concern. They let you kill me and I know it's your fault.

*You still attract me, and I miss you with every passing day, but each day it's eas-
ier. Slowly I tear your fingers from my throat, and slowly I can breathe again. I
don't need you now, and I will never need you again. I did need you then, but
that time is over. I am in control of me, not you. You are strong, and the fight is
hard, but I've seen what you can do and the damage you have done, and I will
not let you do that to me again.*

Sincerely,

"Bill"

Who is a friend of ED?
(A lot more folks than you'd think!)

*"I was a very unattractive child and was reminded about it all the time.
I found much pleasure in eating. It made me feel good. When I became
an adolescent, I started gaining weight. I heard the comments and the
giggles. I was the one girl who was left standing at dances. I was the one
who was bypassed for teams."*

—Anonymous ED sufferer

In the United States, as many as ten million females and one million males
are fighting a life and death battle with an eating disorder such as Anorexia
Nervosa (AN) or Bulimia Nervosa (BN). Approximately twenty-five million
more are struggling with binge eating disorder (BED), according to the
National Eating Disorders Association (NEDA).

Because of the secretiveness and shame associated with eating disorders,
many cases are likely not reported. In addition, many individuals struggle with
body dissatisfaction and sub-clinical disordered eating attitudes and behaviors:

- It has been shown that 80 percent of American women are dissatisfied
  with their appearance (Smolak, 1996).

- For females between fifteen and twenty-four years old, the mortality
  rate associated with anorexia nervosa is twelve times higher than the
  death rate of all other causes of death (Sullivan, 1995).

- Anorexia nervosa has the highest premature fatality rate of any mental
  illness (Sullivan, 1995).

In a 2003 review of the literature on eating disorders, Hoek and van Hoeken found the following:

- Forty percent of newly identified cases of anorexia are in girls fifteen to nineteen years old.

- There have been significant increases in incidence of anorexia from 1935 to 1989, especially among young women age fifteen to twenty-four.

- A rise in incidence of anorexia in young women ages fifteen to nineteen has taken place in each decade since 1930.

- The incidence of bulimia in ten- to thirty-nine-year-old women tripled between 1988 and 1993.

- Only one-third of people with anorexia in the community receive mental health care.

- Only 6 percent of people with bulimia receive mental health care.

- The majority of people with severe eating disorders do not receive adequate care.

Despite its prevalence, there is inadequate research funding for eating disorders. Funding for eating disorders research is approximately 75 percent less than that for Alzheimer's disease. Research dollars spent on eating disorders averaged $1.20 per affected individual, compared to $159.00 per affected individual for schizophrenia.

In March, 2005, NEDA contracted with Global Market Insite, Inc. (GMI), a leader in global market research, to conduct a nationwide sample of 1,500 adults in the U.S. Their findings concluded the following from those surveyed:

- Three out of four Americans believe eating disorders should be covered by insurance companies just like any other illness.

- Americans believe that government should require insurance companies to cover the treatment of eating disorders.

- Four out of ten Americans have either suffered or have known someone who has suffered from an eating disorder.

The media plays a huge role in the prominence of eating disorders, particularly with the current trend toward pro-anorexia (pro-Ana) sites. The following statistics reveal more about the prevalence of disordered eating:

- Over one-half of teenage girls and nearly one-third of teenage boys use unhealthy weight control behaviors such as skipping meals, fasting, smoking cigarettes, vomiting, and taking laxatives (Neumark-Sztainer, 2005).

- Girls who diet frequently are twelve times as likely to binge as girls who don't diet (Neumark-Sztainer, 2005).

- Forty-two percent of first through third grade girls want to be thinner (Collins, 1991).

- Eighty-one percent of ten-year-olds are afraid of being fat (Mellin et al., 1991).

- The average American woman is 5'4" tall and weighs 140 pounds. The average American model is 5'11" tall and weighs 117 pounds.

- Most fashion models are thinner than 98 percent of American women (Smolak, 1996).

- Forty-six percent of nine- to eleven-year-olds are "sometimes" or "very often" on diets, and 82 percent of their families are "sometimes" or "very often" on diets (Gustafson-Larson and Terry, 1992).

- Ninety-one percent of women recently surveyed on a college campus had attempted to control their weight through dieting; twenty-two percent dieted "often" or "always" (Kurth et al., 1995).

- Ninety-five percent of all dieters will regain their lost weight in one to five years (Grodstein et al., 1996).

- Thirty-five percent of "normal dieters" progress to pathological dieting. Of those, twenty to twenty-five percent progress to partial or full-syndrome eating disorders (Shisslak and Crago, 1995).

- Twenty-five percent of American men and forty-five percent of American women are on a diet on any given day (Smolak, 1996).

- Americans spend over $40 billion on dieting and diet-related products each year (Smolak, 1996).

Letters to ED, to our bodies, to ourselves:

Dear ED,

I hate you! You ruined my life. All I can think about is my body, weight, and food. I cannot truly relax and have fun anymore because you control my thoughts.

You don't allow me to ever like anything about myself. It sucks! The only thoughts I have are negative and mean. They are always in my mind.

I want my life back. I want to be able to relax, like myself, and not worry about my body. I want to be normal and be like my friends. I want to enjoy eating, but you ED, you do not allow me to do any of that. I FREAKING HATE YOU, ED and as much as I want to be skinny, it isn't as important as living a happy life.

So, adios ED. I know it will be hard to say good-bye to you, but I am willing to work at it!

Yours in health,

"Katrina"

CHAPTER 1

Are You Friends with Ana, Mia, and Ed?

"I think that the single most important thing is the way society and the media portray body image. We are given the message, over and over and over, that if you are not attractive, forget it, you are a loser. And attractive means thin. My parents never bugged me about my weight, except I liked it when they were concerned that I was too skinny. Maybe I was looking for attention from them."

—Anonymous ED sufferer

I am a therapist for sufferers of ED.

I also suffer from ED.

If that combination seems strange to you, consider this: Have you ever smelled smoke on your family physician's lab coat? Did you ever have a PE coach who was, well, a little zaftig? Have you ever heard a professor mispronounce a word? Or have you ever met a financial planner who couldn't balance her own checkbook?

My point here is that we are all human, and, in my experience, eating disorders, or EDs, are an entirely human experience. They arise out of human thoughts, feelings, and experiences: parents who don't want their kids to grow up "fat," boyfriends who want you to lose weight, and movie stars who are so afraid the camera adds ten pounds that they lose thirty or forty "just to be sure."

You don't catch ED like you catch a cold; in fact, you don't catch it at all. EDs fester over time, growing in response to emotional turmoil that becomes harder and harder to control as you grow up and head out into a world that merely reinforces what you learned at home, at school, or on TV: to be heavy is to be disenfranchised, un-cool, unattractive, and undesirable.

> *I was worthless; I was fat. I was so worthless and so fat I wasn't allowed to eat in front of my grandmother. I loved my grandmother, so she must have been right to not allow me to be so gluttonous.*
> *I was worthless …*

Society reinforces our verbal cues

The messages aren't always verbal. Any woman will tell you that the most stylish clothes are those made for size 8 and under. And any guy can point out where the "regular clothes" end and the "husky" ones begin. (There, right around the corner, next to the broken mannequins and rack of extra hangers.)

We know instinctively where the cool, trendy, upscale, fashionable, fun eateries are. Just as surely, we know exactly what the patrons of such eateries look like and, more importantly, the reception they'd give us if we tried to break the invisible barrier that seems to exist at the front door.

Can't you see them now, even as you're reading this? Can't you picture the look they'd give you if you tried to walk in, get a table, and order a plate of fried chicken and a milkshake? The eye-rolls, the fake smiles, the squeak of chair against floor as they unconsciously—or even quite consciously—shifted away from you?

> *I was worthless; I was fat. I was so worthless and so fat my uncle would force me to exercise to the point of physical exhaustion until I was gagging on my own bile. Then pulling me up by my pony tail, he'd force me to keep working out. I adored my uncle, so he must have been right to force me to continue despite my physical injuries and vomiting.*
> *I was worthless …*

The media's role

Of course, ED messages are directly reinforced in the media. Beyond the heroin thin models and the starving teen actresses, Hollywood pokes fun at what many call America's last socially-approved stereotype.

How do teen dramas portray the bully most likely to injure the most nerds? He's the bulky, husky, apple-cheeked jock, of course, complete with size XXL varsity jacket and double-wide belt.

Who will hold the hand of the painfully thin teen queen starlet when the equally pasty teen stud breaks her heart? The chunky best friend—she of the teddy-bear PJs, comfy pillows, non-ringing phone, and well-stocked fridge.

Need I go on? I could, you know. We all know because we all see it, day in and day out. We see the roles given to those who don't fit the Barbie and Ken mold of LA, NY, and South Beach. This is not news; in fact, it is far from it. I merely point it out to remind you that it's not your fault if you feel bad about your body.

Frankly, I'm surprised anyone in America feels good about their bodies at all!

> *I was worthless; I was fat. I was so worthless and fat that my mother used to make me finish everything on my plate, or I wasn't allowed to go out to play. I loved my mother, so I obeyed, and I ate every morsel on my plate. She must have been right to make me eat when I wasn't hungry.*
> *I was worthless ...*

The real truth behind "the magic number"

Do *you* feel good?
Do you feel worth more?
Or worth *less*?

I think I know the answers to those questions. I know that *you* know the answers. I know you probably scoffed when you read the title of this book: *It's Not About the Weight!* That's because, to you, it's all about the weight.

It's all about that magic number in your head. What is it this week? 103? 99? 82? What was it last week? Or the week before? Can you remember the number you started at when your journey with Ana, Mia, or Ed began?

I bet you can. I bet this is also true: even if you reach that new number, it's not going to be enough for you—103 will still be too much. So you'll set your sights on 99, but when you reach that, it will still be too much. So you'll set your sights on 82, but when you … well, you get the picture. That's how you got to 103 in the first place.

So why? Why is there no magic number to make you smile? Why, when you starve yourself to go from triple digits to double digits, are you still not satisfied? Why are there no digits on the scale to make you jump for joy? Why, if it's all about the weight, does no single weight satisfy you?

Try this little experiment: imagine there were no scales to define your weight. If you couldn't tell whether you weigh 130 or 103, would that make you happy? And if the fashion designers of the world all got together and decided to do away with sizes altogether and everyone in the world was required to wear the same bland, sizeless, boring thing, what would you do then? How could you compare your size—your worth—with others? You would find some other way to measure your weight—to measure yourself. You'd use other numbers, like waist size or tape measures.

My point? Weight, size, shape—none of it matters. Your ED springs from within, not without. It was created in your brain by being told time and time again that fat was bad or weight mattered or size defined you, and over time you slowly began to believe that you could control *how you felt* with *how you looked.*

How's that working out for you so far?

> *I was worthless; I was fat. I was so worthless and so fat that I realized I had to change. I wanted to eat with my grandmother, and I wanted to be thin for my uncle, and I wanted to keep the peace with my mother. I just wanted to be loved by all of them. One day I chose to alter my life. I loved and adored myself, so I must have been right to change my life.*

Reaching the masses

The bottom line is this: I have an eating disorder. I'm happy now, I'm healthy, I look good and feel good—yes, I even feel good about how I look—but I did have, still have, and will always have an ED. That makes it especially easy for me to counsel others with EDs, and particularly hard for me as well. I know that there but for the grace of God go I, and every patient who ever sits across from me is a mirror for my own insecurities, shame, pride, ego, dread, hope, and fear.

Their stories are my stories; their nightmares are my nightmares. I can't hug a seventy-five-pound teenager without remembering myself at that age. I remember how confused I was and how sad and broken and scared and lonely

I felt. I remember how my closet was my enemy, and every time I opened the fridge it became all-out warfare.

And, I have to admit, I'm tired—tired of counseling patients only to turn them back over to those who would unintentionally perpetuate their disease. I'm tired of rushing to the ER to counsel a family as another patient clings to life, unable to go on living on 500 calories a day and unwilling to eat anymore. I'm tired of watching reality shows that glamorize plastic surgery and rail-thin models as beautiful. I'm tired of running across more and more Web sites devoted solely to "eating disorder chic," or the perpetuation of "bony as beauty."

That's why I wrote this book. I can counsel up to fifty individual patients and their families every week for the rest of my life and never get enough of the message across, but with this book I can reach forty-five thousand people in a single printing! It's going to take a lot of printings to cover the spread; In the United States, as many as ten million females and one million males are fighting a life and death battle with an eating disorder such as anorexia or bulimia. Approximately twenty-five million more are struggling with binge eating disorder (Crowther et al., 1992; Fairburn et al., 1993; Gordon, 1990; Hoek, 1995; Shisslak et al., 1995). That adds up to some thirty-six million people are affected by EDs in this country alone, That's no typo: thirty-six million.

There is a reason you are reading this book. There has to be. Anorexia, bulimia, binge eating, recovery rates, and deadly statistics aren't exactly stimulating reading material, right? Maybe it's you who has the relationship with ED, or perhaps it is your daughter, son, sister, best friend, classmate, student, teacher, co-worker, or neighbor?

The thing about ED is that it touches all of us. I can never counsel a single member of a family without affecting the entire family. What's worse is that if I don't counsel anyone else in that family I am basically sending my patient home to the enemy. It sounds harsh, but oftentimes families are not only the root cause of the ED but at times, the codependent enabler of the ED as well.

Think about where your first thoughts, philosophies, fears, foibles, and feelings about ED originated. They may have come from sitting around the dinner table with your folks, right? You were affected by comments such as, "You eat too much" or "Better not have that second helping. You don't want to end up like your brother Ralphie, do you?" Our parents do more harm than they could ever imagine.

It's not their fault, of course. Parents don't want to plant the seeds of future therapy; it's not their intent to send their kids rushing to do that which they've just warned them not to do. I've yet to meet a parent who consciously wanted to give their child an eating disorder.

However, the barbs add up, the jokes blossom, the nicknames stick, and the dinner table becomes a nightly battlefield. What started out as a young child with a tendency to overeat or gain weight in all the "wrong places," or who was simply not out of their baby fat years yet, slowly transforms into a very unhappy, self-conscious, guilty, and vulnerable young adult.

Recipe for an eating disorder

I always tell my clients that if there was a recipe for forming an eating disorder, all of the basic ingredients—guilt, shame, insecurity, low self-esteem, perfectionism, passive-aggressiveness, pride, ego—are already a part of a very fragile psyche.

What may become precipitated at home slowly gets reinforced over time by others of the same opinion. Your girlfriends snicker about the fat girls at school. Your buddies spend an inordinate amount of time thinking up clever nicknames for the school hefties. Upperclassmen fan the flames while, in turn, you watch as your peers pick on the greenhorns coming up behind you.

Yes, kids can be cruel, but some adults are just as vicious. There's the PE coach who openly heckles the overweight kids on the bench or who subconsciously excludes them by picking the most athletic kids to be captains of the team. There's the cafeteria worker who puts less on your plate than on the plates of the other kids, or the teacher who makes cracks about the new kid's waist size.

The converse is also true: the bigger the child, the bigger the plate, until the vicious cycle continues to repeat itself. As a heftier kid, people often think you need more to eat, not less, and pile your plate even higher.

"Waste not, want not," the saying goes. As I've mentioned before, pleasing people and EDs go hand in hand. As "pleasers-in-training," many husky children feel compelled to finish all that is on their plate. So if the dinner table is not a battlefield because people are calling you fat, it becomes one as good hosts and hostesses try to accommodate you!

Home and school are not the only breeding grounds for body image derailment. What about the candy store clerk who "cuts you off" after a few candy bars, the local hoods who shout insults from their car windows as they pass, or the beloved neighbor who has a nickname for everyone, usually to reflect the opposite of how they appear. The town giant is "Tiny," the city octogenarian is "Youngin," and you're "Slim," nicknamed with a know-it-all grin.

I was worthless; I was fat—you have been reading these italicized words throughout this chapter. Those are my words. I lived them; I wrote them. Do they sound familiar? Have you felt worthless in the past? Do you feel worthless now? As you read this passage are you feeling as if this is all just … so … hopeless? Are you wishing you could just fast forward to health and be done with it? Are you thinking these words would mean so much more to you if only you were five, ten, fifteen, or fifty pounds thinner?

I hope not. I hope that you're ready for change. I hope that you are ready for the kind of massive, hard, and lasting change that comes from reading the right book—or meeting the right person—at just the right time.

I hope this is that time for you.

I hope that this is the right book—that I am the right person—for you.

No matter where you are, who you are, what you look like, what size you wear, how much you weigh, or what ED you have, I can help. I know I can help because this morning I helped someone just like you, and later this afternoon I will help another someone just like you.

That is what I do. The road ahead won't be easy. I'd be lying if I told you otherwise. It won't be easy because no matter what ED you have or how much weight you've lost or feel you need to lose or might have even gained back, eating disorders are serious business; it is life or death stuff.

Healing from something that could kill you? It is hard work; there is no doubt about it. But it is work that lasts, and it is work that you need. You can't do it on your own. I've seen too many people try—try and fail. That's because you're not out of the woods just because you gain back some weight or keep down one more egg white than yesterday.

You know why? Because *It's Not About the Weight*! That's not just a clever title, tag line or brand name; it's the truth. Your disease—and that's what it is, a disease—starts deep inside. It's at the core of who you are, what you do, how you look, what you eat, when you eat, how much you eat, and most definitely why you eat. You already know it. If eating was only hunger-related, we'd all look like the hunters and gatherers that were our ancestors. We'd eat until we were full and no more. We'd eat when we were hungry and not again until we were hungry again. But that's not how it is, is it?

My health is your health

That's because *It's Not About the Weight*. It's about the pain, the fear, the insecurity, the emotions and the shame that drive your eating. Or not eating. Or bingeing. Or purging. Or simply just your attitude toward food, weight or body image in general. Remember, you don't have to look like you have anorexia nervosa to have an ED. How you look is insignificant compared to what's going on deep inside.

I say I still have an ED because my thoughts and feelings about food and my body image at times haunt me the same way they did when I was a young girl, a teenager, a young woman, and later a grown woman. I just manage those thoughts and feelings differently today.

You think taking my author's photo for this book was easy? No, friends, the feelings about food and body image never go away entirely. We have to work on that, and we will, but for now I want to make one thing perfectly clear: food is neither your enemy nor your friend. Food is just food. The scale does not like you better when you are thin than it does when you are heavier. The scale is a tool. It is a piece of metal and plastic with a window and a dial and some numbers that mean absolutely nothing. That is all. It doesn't smile or frown, laugh behind your back, or look forward to your presence.

This is not a diet, a workbook, a meal plan, or a calorie expander. This is a story with a lesson—nothing more, nothing less. The story is mine, and the lesson is mine. The story will sound very familiar; the lesson will hopefully be something new, but just as easily understood.

At the beginning of this introduction I asked you, "Are You Friends with Ana, Mia, and Ed?" It was a trick question. Ana, Mia, and Ed aren't real people, of course. Ana stands for anorexia. (Cute, huh?) Mia? Can you guess? Mia is slim-speak for bulimia. (Clever, right?) And I've already explained how ED stands for eating disorders. But that's not the trick; the real trick in my trick question was how Ana, Mia and Ed make millions upon millions of people feel like they are not just their friends, but their best friends!

Ana makes you feel beautiful, right?

Mia keeps you on track.

And ED? Well, ED embraces you in a dozen different ways a day.

These cute names, these pro-Ana Web sites, this treatment backlash that has become so popular today are full of trick questions just like mine. They ask you to believe the opposite of what is true, which is a trick by any definition. They ask you to believe that unhealthy is healthy, painful is pretty, and bony is beautiful. They urge you to believe them, not your therapist, doctor, teachers, parents, family, or friends.

But I know better, and soon you will, too: Ana, Mia and Ed are not your friends.

They never were.

They never will be.

> *I am not worthless, and my body is healthy. I now manage my life and live for me, no matter what my size, no matter what my weight, no matter what my shape (and believe me, they all fluctuate). My body loves me for nourishing it, and I love my body!*

The opposite of "worth less" is …?

"I was worthless," I said in my earlier quotes.

That's because, for a very long time, that's how I felt: worthless. Not worth more, not even worth a little, but worth *less*. I felt worth less than my parents, my siblings, my friends, my classmates, my boyfriends, my teachers, my neighbors, and my peers. I felt worth less than those models in the magazines, the stars on TV, the popular kids at my school, and the girl next to me in the dressing room. I felt worth less than the people waiting on me at the restaurants where I'd drown my feelings of being worth less than everybody else in more and more food or, depending on my ED of the month, less and less.

How about you? Have you felt worthless lately?

I don't want you to feel worthless anymore. I want you to feel worth *more*! If I share nothing else with you as we journey through this book together, I want you to feel more worth by the time the journey is over.

You are not worth less.

You are worth more than you know.

Now it's time to show you why …

Letters to ED, to our bodies, to ourselves:

Dear Ed,

Your words are harsh; they scream at me. I'm never doing it right. You turned my self-esteem meter all the way down to "everyone's staring," "you're not good enough," "you're too fat to wear that." My once self-loving mind has been put to sleep, and you have taken over, basically my life.

Your words overpower every move I make—thinking how many more calories I'll burn if I tap my feet in class, convincing myself I'm not hungry when my stomach is growling.

And it's not just me you've taken over. It's pretty crazy how you can be in so many heads at once, telling us all what to do, ruining our lives. You're like the murderer who can't be caught, can't be killed, can't even be seen. I wish I knew what satisfaction you got from this. The only answer that comes to mind is having so many people fall in love with you, obsess over you and do what you say.

We met about a year ago—the first summer I began to hate myself in a bathing suit. I used you as my outlet ... I loved food too much, so you and I would just throw it all up, no big deal. You started to take lunch away from me, and as time continued, food became my enemy. It was all I could think about all the time, literally. I'm pathetic, and I have you to blame. I can barely remember what life was like before you, and now I'm scared to let you go.

You've done permanent damage to my mind and body, and you've convinced me that life without you is not the one for me. I hate the money my mom has to spend and the fun I've missed while hating myself. You've been by my side through everything, and a tiny part of me is thankful. The other part wants to say good-bye, make a new best friend, and feel what it's like to be normal again.

I'm scared to believe I have to, and I don't believe I can. I want to be at the point where I want to try for ME, not for everyone else. I don't care if you kill me, but I know my friends and family do. I don't care if I become skin and bones, but the people around me will wonder.

You're forcing me to be so selfish, that I don't even care about the people who care about me. You fucked me up, made life hell, but with you in my head that doesn't bother me. All I want is to be sicker, sicker, sick. Fuck you Ed, leave me alone. I love you Ed, please don't go.

Sincerely,

"Leslie"

CHAPTER 2

When Your Social Life Turns Deadly

(Social Learning and Why We Act the Way We Do)

"For boys, the family was the place from which one sprang and to which one returned for comfort and support, but the field of action was the larger world of wilderness, adventure, industry, labor, and politics. For girls, the family was to be the world, their field of action the domestic circle. He was to express himself in his work and, through it and social action, was to help transform his environment; her individual growth and choices were restricted to lead her to express herself through love, wifehood, and motherhood—through the support and nurture of others, who would act for her."

—Gerda Lerner, author of *The Female Experience*

When I was a young teen, I had a slew of issues, but no one, including me, knew it was all really part of an eating disorder. No one knew what an eating disorder was back then. In my day, kids ate, grew up, ate, lost their baby fat, and still ate. If they didn't lose their baby fat, they ate less or got more active and everything worked out fine. At least this is what the happy, healthy families on *Leave it to Beaver* and the *Facts of Life* would have us believe.

But out in the real world, things were quite a bit different. I'm not here to lay blame; it wasn't really anybody's fault—least of all my own, my parents, or my friends—that what was essentially ED got misdiagnosed as, well, basically everything else.

My symptoms were depression, irritability, poor grades, moodiness, self-loathing, and a list of other prickly behaviors. Of course, my mom didn't believe kids could be depressed. Today, it is common knowledge that children, in fact, have somatic (or body) complaints such as headaches and other pains because they can't verbalize their very real, very clinical depression.

But I verbalized my depression; I wrote lots of angry, sad, depressed poetry that I used to hang on the walls in dark, deep calligraphy, framed in blacks and browns. It was there to remind me of just how miserably unhappy I really was.

Mom used to come upstairs and tell me I was a wonderful writer, especially of poems, but would always undo her positive praise by asking, "Can't you write anything happy for a change?" That was her response. It was clear that she just didn't get it! I mean, c'mon Mom. Don't you see that your daughter is depressed? Suicidal? What does it take? I need help, Mom! Of course I can't write happy poems! I'm troubled!

Thank goodness my writing was my outlet. I never once remember her asking me about any of the poems, although looking back on that period—and my covered walls—I was darkly disturbed.

The long list of doctors begins

After I acted out one too many times, Mom took me to, of all things, a gynecologist. Her feeling was always that medical doctors were somehow safer and better than psychologists. God forbid her precious daughter had a "mental problem."

But why a gynecologist? I suppose Mom's thinking at the time was that my depression had something to do with becoming a woman. Naturally, a visit to the gynecologist proved futile; everything was just fine, anatomically speaking. And even though the visit was more physical than psychological, I consider that first trip to be Doctor #1 in a long line of visits that would prove to be of little help in diagnosing my ED or my depression, let alone curing it.

Naturally, my depression gradually deepened. I ate more, I ate less, and while outwardly my ED symptoms were still manageable, inside a battle was raging. Finally, right before we moved from Milwaukee to Syracuse just before my sixteenth birthday, Mom took me to see Doctor #2, an actual child psychologist.

I can't imagine how much this vexed my mother to actually call a child psychologist and make an appointment for her precious child. It was a bone of contention with Mom that her precious child could have a problem. Why, our family was perfect! What could ever possibly be wrong? (It certainly couldn't have been anything *she* caused.) But she did call him; I've got to give her credit for that.

After a bit of testing ("Where does the sun rise? Repeat these numbers after me. Put these pictures in order …"), he told my mother, with me standing there, *right in front of him*: "Your daughter will never be college bound. She will always be an average or below average student, and you must put her in a remedial high school when you move to New York. She needs special attention. Never expect anything much from her. She buckles under pressure."

And that, as they say, was that.

Talk about being a fly on the wall for your own funeral. Could my already low self-esteem have gotten any lower at that point? Worse still, his words echoed through the next two decades of my life, overshadowing any joy I might have felt that would have helped battle the constant depression. Many times I thought he'd been exactly right.

Only my internal nature would prevail. My maternal grandfather had been universally referred to as "stubborn as a mule," and some of that trait trickled down through the emotion, the pain, and the hurt to keep me protectively sealed off from the kind of professional and systemic abuse I was receiving at the hands of the profession I would eventually call my own.

I know without a doubt that I wouldn't be a doctor today, let alone writing this book, were it not for that stubborn streak and a driving will to grit my teeth and grind through the process of school, work, health, and happiness even while the rest of my brain was shrieking, "That doctor was right; you'll never be good enough, you're too ugly, too fat, too stupid, too fragile, ready to crumble at a moment's notice …"

Unfortunately, however, at that time positive mental health was still many, many years in the future and, with no light at the end of the tunnel, I made preparations for moving day. With Doctor #2's recommendations still ringing in my ears, it was off to Syracuse, leaving my boyfriend behind in Milwaukee—the "nice one" and the only real source of salvation I ever felt up until that time in my nearly sixteen years on the planet.

"Say hello to my little friend …"

Did my depression worsen? You bet. Alone, at a new school, scared, and more insecure than ever, and knowing I could never be normal according to the so-called child psychologist, I was forced to adjust the only way I knew how.

So, what did I do? How did I adjust? What was my coping mechanism? I started to take back control. I realized that nobody outside of me—no parents, doctors, friends, or boyfriends—could help me. So, it was up to me. Only I could help myself. But what was in my control?

I was a kid, barely sixteen, living in a strange place, with no car, no money, no job, no education, and no confidence. Who, or what, could I control under such limited circumstances? Then it hit me one day: food! I could decide what went in—or more specifically, what went out—of my body. How much, how little, what, when, and how it got in there were really the only things under my control.

And control felt good. It didn't just feel good; it felt great! For the first time I had control over something. Other people could tell me what to do, but whenever I wanted, I could turn control on or off; hunger became less an enemy and more a friend.

Saying "no" to dessert empowered me. Walking away from an unfinished meal felt sublime. I wasn't useless; I *could* amount to something, after all. (Take that, Doctor #2!) I didn't crack under pressure. I could face hunger and not just succeed but triumph over it. Even when everyone else was scarfing down pizza and cookies and my stomach was literally growling I could prevail; I could succeed.

In other words, I met my new best friend: ED.

Life with ED

First I restricted. Or, at least, I tried to restrict. I wasn't alone, of course. I still lived under Mom's thumb and it was usually covered with spaghetti sauce, chocolate, or potato chips!

Mealtime was a game of strategy: how could I eat the least amount of food without offending Mom? Mom loved to force feed; it was a generational (well, OK, a love) thing. Kids might starve in Europe, but not in her house. Heck, she fed the entire neighborhood, too. She never caught on to the liver or the brisket squashed tightly in my napkin as I headed for the garbage can in the garage.

At home, Mom was old school; what went on your plate went in your gullet. "Your father works hard all day to put that food on your plate," she would always say. "Clean your plate. There are starving kids in Europe." I used to think to myself, "Well then, send the food to them." If you didn't eat, Mom thought you could just sit there and wait until you got hungry again. It didn't do to undereat at Mom's table, so I had to eat just to make her happy and keep her out of my hair.

Along with overstuffed meals came another inevitability: purging. With Mom's watchful eye hovering over every mouthful, I could eat to my heart's content and still have control: the minute we were free to leave the table I hit the farthest bathroom away from the kitchen, where Mom still had another hour of cleaning to do. Plenty of time to empty my stomach of dinner, not to mention whatever was leftover from lunch and my after-school snack. (Or so I thought.)

Mom wasn't my only worry during those Syracuse days; the move had brought us just down the street from my grandmother. Unlike Mom, "Nana" as we called her, had a completely opposite philosophy when it came to food: less is more.

Mom might have had me on a "see food" diet, but *her* mom was from another generation entirely. Nana firmly believed that thin was in, and where Mom piled my plate with endless helpings, Nana's servings started small and got smaller along the way. The more you ate at one house meant the less you ate at the other! And so I learned to know my audience: eat/overeat or binge/purge at home with Mom and starve at Nana's.

Somehow I managed to get through high school without killing myself. My depression was far from gone, however, and my ED was in full bloom. It wasn't until two years later when I went away to college that ED and I *really* got to know each other.

College daze

Despite what Doctor #2 had said only two years earlier, by age seventeen I had been accepted to the University of Miami in Florida to study—get this—Engineering and Architecture! And, since Mom said I needed to have a "normal" college life, I went away to the first college that accepted me. Was it likely I would have a normal college life in Miami, Florida? Ha! If you only knew Mom!

I think Mom was just afraid I would buckle under the pressure of trying to get into other schools (just as the doctor had said two years before). Oh well, I hated myself so much, and I actually wanted to get as far away from what I thought was a family who despised me so much, that off I went to Miami … all alone. That was the farthest thing from normal I could have ever experienced. There is *nothing* normal about Miami, Florida, at least not for an uncultured, naïve, seventeen-year-old kid from the Midwest! But it was the best thing ED could have asked for.

I was alone, and my power was quickly deteriorating. There was no Mom at the dinner table to binge/purge for and no Nana to starve myself for. But I quickly found other ways to torture myself, and my power flitted in and out of reach for the first few months in Miami.

Here was a world of beautiful people: models, model wannabes, aerobics instructors, and gym rats. The only thing they loved better than all that bright Florida sunshine was themselves. Immediately I started comparing myself to them: my body, my life, my parents, my smarts, my height, my face, my bone structure, my hair, my siblings, my father's job, my socio-economic status, my thighs, and my waist. Get the point? I hated me! I hated everything about me!

Everyone was (or appeared to be on the surface) happy, skinny, rich, pretty, and about thirty pounds lighter than I was. I hated it; I hated myself, I hated my classes, and I hated my choice of college. In short, I hated life.

And the only way to deal with that hatred was to regain some power and get back some control. And so, unbidden, I starved myself, and then I starved some more. Then, just to make sure I was good and powerful, I starved a whole lot more.

But the starving wasn't working on its own. No matter how hungry I got, no matter how much I resisted, I just wasn't good enough. So I did something I'd never done before: I joined a gym.

Problem was, I didn't have a car. So I begged, borrowed, and got to the gym any way I could. Once there I worked out three to four hours every morning, seven days a week. Suddenly, I was power personified. I could starve myself and exert myself to near death. How awesome was that?

Of course, the comparisons never stopped. I wouldn't go out with anyone. Why? Because I *had* to work out. It was the only way to stay powerful and to keep control. I *had* to take two aerobics classes in a row and do my weights for the first half of every day. There was just no time for anything—or any-one—else.

I didn't want anyone else anyway. I didn't even want me. Every hour at the gym was punishment for sins not committed but entirely felt and for self-hatred that consumed me. I looked in the mirror only to see my progress, not to stare at the face I could no longer stand.

I compared myself to everyone and everything, and I always wound up short. All those people in the gym, all those hours every day, and I spoke to no one and no one spoke to me. I had one friend and one friend only: ED. But ED didn't exist back then, remember?

Miami vice

There was no diagnosis for my insatiable hunger to starve; there was no name to put on my irrational behavior. I knew only control, power, and release. I needed to control something—anything! Miami was so huge and the people were so pretty; my classes were so hard and I was so painfully, heartbreakingly alone. The only way to survive was to return to the one place I knew I could find peace: starvation, hunger, shame, and guilt.

The worst part was that I was alone in all of this. I felt like a freak. No one could eat this little and survive, right? Day after day the pressure intensified, and so day after day I needed to do more of what I hated about myself in the first place: less food, more exercise, and less free time. No one would ever understand, so I had no one to talk to.

Well, that wasn't entirely true: I called home every Sunday as expected. I told Mom that I wanted to transfer to the University of Florida. I knew that Miami wasn't a healthy atmosphere for me. Oh, but Mom (and ED) insisted I stay. I complained about the other girls at school: their beauty and mystique and bodies and physique. You know what Mom said when I told her about all of the pretty, rich, and skinny girls? I know she was really trying to be helpful at the time, but what she said was, "Susie, those are the girls that boys want to be seen with, but *you're* the kind of girl who a boy will want to settle down with and marry one day."

Even at my age of forty-three right now, this very day as I write this book, I cannot get that statement out of my head. I mean, what kind of a back-handed compliment is that anyway?

"OK, Mom. So, I'm ugly, fat, and no one wants to be seen with me in the prime of my life, but I have every other quality that any man would just love. So if I could just wait a few years I'll be in demand?" This was *not* what an eighteen-year-old wanted to hear. Not what any woman—at any age—wants to hear. Did Mom never see how my body was shrinking away?

Now, don't get me wrong: Mothers didn't know about these things, especially in the 1980s. So, Mom, if you're reading this, there is something you should know: I am not, in any way, blaming you. I know that you did your best, as all parents do. You didn't know; you *couldn't* have known. Even the doctors you dragged me to didn't know.

But that's exactly why I am writing this book with such passion. I want other parents, coaches, doctors, nurses, teachers, and adults in general to know how these comments can permeate our psyches and do impenetrable damage for years and years and years. Some of us never recover. And there is little hope of recovery without professional help.

Three strikes you're out, or what's behind Doctor #3?

Of course, I tried to recover in my own way. Years passed; the power—and the weight—came and went. I fasted, I feasted, I starved, and I purged. Along the way my very identity fused with food; it was who I was and what I did and how I did and all that mattered.

Along the way, I lost myself.

Along the way, I saw Doctor #3.

The third doctor that I visited was after I had checked myself into the hospital after attempting to kill myself at the age of twenty-three. She walked into my hospital room and told me to use my hands to express how big I thought I was. Naturally, I held my hands out as far and wide as I possibly could.

Rather than seeing that as a big warning sign, she walked out of the hospital room and I never saw her again. No one ever addressed my body image issues with me, nor provided therapy to me for anything called an eating disorder. They treated me for depression, but completely ignored ED. They gave me some pills that didn't work (in fact, they made me feel twice as bad), because I still hated myself, my body and my life ... and in the end nobody understood me ... *still.*

Still feeling like a genetic mutant (but always making myself look perfect on the outside), I worked as a Director of Therapeutic Recreation in a rehabilitation hospital. Suicide attempt or not, I was your typical ambitious, driven, hard working, type-A personality.

Despite the busy work and the degrees and the titles and the certificates, I couldn't stave off the inevitable misery, and a couple of years later I went to see another doctor (#4; are you keeping track?), this time a man. I sat in his office, waiting for nearly half an hour after my scheduled appointment time, until he finally came in to see me, winded from an afternoon jog. (He wasn't late because of another patient or a medical emergency, but due to *his* compulsive afternoon-jog around the block! How's that for making me feel good about myself?)

Without apologizing for his tardiness—and still wearing his running shoes as he sweated all over me—he told me that I'd feel "fine" if I would only "start exercising." That was *his* prescription: good, old-fashioned exercise. A cure for the mind and body, he suggested.

Exercise? *That* was his prescription? If only he knew that I belonged to a twenty-four-hour gym. So in addition to the two hours I worked out during every day, I'd usually get up in the middle of the night feeling I hadn't exercised enough! What was my remedy? Another two hours in the gym during the middle of the night! So exercise obviously wasn't my problem.

I never went back to see him, either.

There never was a Doctor #5—well, not for a long time to come, as far as ED was concerned. There was no medical center devoted to EDs, no wing of any medical center devoted to EDs (but, then again, I didn't even know I had an ED), and no doctor who specialized in anything but diets (a short-term fix and the root of most of my problems in the first place) and quick weight-loss schemes (a scam, then and now).

In many ways, going to see those four doctors made my problems worse. I grew more isolated, certain that no one in my area could help me and more convinced than ever that I truly was a freak of nature. If there was no one to treat this disease, then surely no one else in the entire country was suffering from it.

I gave up, gave in, and spiraled out of control for most of the next two decades, waiting for science to catch up with me. Twenty years ago, these were my therapeutic options: Doctor #1 (she's healthy); Doctor #2 (she needs special schooling because she'll never amount to anything); Doctor #3 (pills and discharge from the hospital); Doctor #4 (exercise and you'll feel much better); none of which did anything to treat the inner demons driving me to eat, to not eat, to binge, to purge, to not binge, to not purge, to eat, and to not eat some more.

None of those doctors asked me how I felt mentally and emotionally, but solely concentrated on the physical (except for the one who determined I was depressed. No kidding!) None of them talked to my nuclear family to study our dynamics, or asked me to write down what I ate, when I ate, how I felt when I ate, after I ate, before I ate, about what I ate, or simply about the process of eating in general. None of them asked me how I felt about me or my body! I was poked, prodded, prescribed pills, given bad advice, and sent back to the very places where my problems had all started: my family's dinner table, society, my own little private world, and my own warped mind.

That was then, this is how ...

Today the psychiatric pendulum has swung in nearly the opposite direction; not only is there much more information available to today's vulnerable and ED-headed young adult, but at times it can seem like too much information. There are so many books, magazines, issues, reports, surveys, studies, websites, statistics, experts, pseudo-experts, gurus, and mentors that one barely knows where to begin.

Which book is the best? Which ED accurately describes me? Am I anorexic? But I occasionally binge, so I must have compulsive-eating disorder, right? Where's the book on that? But I purge, too, so where does that leave me? Maybe you haven't purged yet, or binged yet, or aren't too skinny or too fat, but your mind is definitely becoming unhealthily preoccupied with food.

Where to turn then?

Where to begin searching?

I'd like to solve that problem right now: we begin at the very start: your childhood, your home, society, and more specifically ...

How we became socialized

Let's face it: you didn't grow up in a vacuum. No matter how insular your formative years might have been, no matter how good your neighborhood or exclusive your schools or strong your parental units or high the fence around your house, you were impacted by modern day American society. Daily. Hourly. For better or worse.

You watched TV, listened to the radio, read the newspaper (OK, the funnies), heard the news, and listened to your parents talk about their very adult, very outside world. Whether you knew the history behind it or the pros and cons, you knew about our society: war, racism, poverty, class segregation, the economy, stocks, bonds, transportation, energy, pollution, third world countries, and our country.

It happened in little ways you could hardly have defined. Women wore dresses and men wore pants. Your teachers made little comments to help you on your way, just in case you forgot: "Janie, stay away from those boys. Football is for men," or "Robby, you don't want to be over there messing with those girls. Hopscotch is for the young ladies ..."

You knew just who to hang out with because they looked just like you, and whom to avoid because, well, they looked like them. What you were by first grade—nerd, jock, popular, unpopular, class clown, troublemaker—was most likely how you stayed because your classmates, even your teachers, were long of memory and short of forgiveness.

Even if you tried to break out of your very strict and socialized role—joining a sport, sitting with the popular kids, losing weight, trading in your glasses for contacts—the reception was such that, before long, you'd give up out of sheer resistance.

"Glad to have you back," said your old nerd friends.

"Stay where you belong," muttered the in-crowd.

Over time, of course, things changed, but not very much. Girls were still girls, boys were still boys, the jocks still played sports, and the girls, well, most didn't. Teachers dropped their little hints, parents dropped them louder, and society snuck in whenever and however it possibly could.

Don't believe me? Let's see if any of this sounds familiar:

That was then …

From birth, boys and girls are socialized differently:

- Boys got the blue.

- Girls got the pink.

- Boys get the trucks.

- Girls get the baby dolls. (Funny, if you think about it, boys get dolls too, but they call them "action figures.")

- Boys learned to support the household financially.

- Girls learned to nurture others.

- Boys aren't supposed to cry.

- Girls let it all out.

- Girls' reported rates of depression are twice that for males. (In my opinion, this is due to reporting error, since boys don't reach out for help.)

- Boys act out aggressively rather than internalize depression.

- Boys are taught to be tough (by not crying).

- Girls are taught that it's "OK" to "look" weak.

- Boys are taught that asking for help is cowardly.

... *This is now*

As we grow, the socialization gradually evolves:

- We have two income families:

  - Women work;

  - Men work.

- Our toys are still different:

  - Girls play with tools that make their home life easier (vacuums, bread makers, closet organizers, compacts); their job easier (laptops, video cell phones, Blackberries), thus fulfilling their complicated dual roles as providers and nurturers;

  - Boys play with bigger toys that make life more fun (boats, ATVs, bigger cells, bigger Blackberries).

- Woman work twice as hard (home, family, occupations) and are expected to do more: look like models, be super-human, etc.

- Men struggle with their emerging roles as "sensitive males," urged to deal more with their emotions but not told how.

It all adds up to one thing: more pressure. Naturally, thanks to our socialization, women react to pressure differently than men. Today women are expected to be both earth mother and breadwinner. Even in families where both parents work the man does less child-rearing than the woman, and traditional roles such as housekeeper and caretaker are still sloshed over into the pile of daily "woman's work."

That doesn't mean that men are immune from more pressure, though. Why? Men have more competition. These days women are out making money and don't *need* men like they used to. More women are living independently now than ever. And men are now turning to their bodies to "look" more masculine or "better" because that's all they can "control" that woman can't compete with them on.

What does this mean? How do pressure, role reversal, and socialization affect eating disorders? For women, what was already an existing problem has been made worse. For men, new concerns about looking good, grooming, staying younger, fitter, and more attractive longer have brought them into the ED fold as never before.

All this from playing with dolls or action figures? Well, not exactly. In this section we are going to be discussing three psychological issues that directly affect your susceptibility to EDs: classical conditioning, operant conditioning, and social learning theory.

Wait, hold on, stop; don't go anywhere: I used to teach this stuff so I know how quickly your eyes glaze over! This is (believe me, I'm going to catch guff from my colleagues) the briefest version possible just to arm you with the knowledge that (a) it's not your fault, (b) it's easier than you thought to overcome, (c) understanding and knowledge are the dual keys to unlock recovery, and (d) the more you recognize that your problems *are* under your control the sooner you'll quit looking to the scale or, worse, self-destructive behaviors, diets, or invasive procedures for help!

Classical conditioning, or what do Pavlov, Spielberg, and yogurt have in common?

The first of our behavioral theories is called classical conditioning, and, while it may sound Greek to you now, stick with me and you'll see that, actually, you are already a master of classical conditioning.

How? Let's listen in: Da dum. Da dum. Da dum, da dum, da dum, da dum. (Man, I wish this book came with a soundtrack!) Recognize it? Well, in case my rhythm is a tad off, it's the theme music from *Jaws*, and back when I taught Psych 101 I would play it as students came into the classroom for our initial discussion of classical conditioning.

Students who had seen the movie knew immediately that something was amiss, trouble was on the way, and doom was just around the corner. Students who'd never seen the movie (the nerve!) merely thought I was in a little need of Psych 101 myself (and maybe not supposed to be teaching it).

But let me break down why the *Jaws* theme is such a perfect illustration of classical conditioning. For starters, a definition: Classical conditioning is an association. By associating one thing with another, we are conditioned to feel or behave in a certain way. Don't be confused by the word conditioned; it's just another way of saying learned. In this case, conditioned behavior equals learned behavior.

For instance, those students who'd seen *Jaws* were conditioned by the music to know that something unpleasant was on the horizon. In the two hours it took them to watch half-a-dozen innocent victims get slaughtered by a rogue Great White they had learned (been conditioned) to associate that "Da dum. Da dum. Da dum, da dum, da dum, da dum" theme with blood, gore, frothy water, screaming, wailing, sinking boats, and general mayhem.

What began merely as notes on a keyboard—Da dum. Da dum. Da dum, da dum, da dum, da dum—became, when played during violent scenes from the film, a "classic" case of classical conditioning: we naturally came to associate the "score with the gore." All those years later my grown college students could still feel impending doom when those familiar notes struck home.

Of course, that's just one modern example. Classical conditioning actually rose to our collective consciousness when a Russian physiologist named Pavlov observed the production of saliva in dogs at feeding time. But let's not ring that old bell; sorry, a little psychologist humor there.

Instead of discussing Pavlov, his dogs, his meat powder, and his bells, let me give you another little modern twist: let's say that you bring home a brand new puppy.

Homecoming is sweet, but eventually it's feeding time, right? Well, when you first open the can of food (otherwise known as a neutral stimulus), the puppy hasn't a clue what the noise is, and he doesn't come running. However, eventually, the puppy realizes that the sound of the can opener is associated with, what else? food! Soon thereafter, every single time the puppy hears that can opener (even if you are opening your own food), he comes running and salivating, ready for that next plate of food.

But dogs, and people, learn; even when they don't realize they are—or even intend to. Let's say that same puppy sees you heading toward the cupboard where you keep the canned food. Before you even open the can, the dog sees you opening the cupboard and he comes running and drooling. What's happened here? How does this classify as classical conditioning? Well, your new puppy has not only associated the can-opener noise with food, but also the cupboard. This causes the same conditioned response/behavior.

Da dum. Da dum. Da dum, da dum, da dum, da dum …

So, Spielberg—or in this case his trusted composer John Williams—merely traded in a familiar keyboard drumming for the sound of a bell, and millions of moviegoers traded in screams, shouts, fainting spells, and a lifelong fear of water for Pavlov's dog's salivation.

The yogurt incident

OK, big deal. What does classical conditioning have to do with *you* and, more specifically, you and your friend ED? Well, I'll use another example to show you what it means to me, and then let's catch up and see if it sounds familiar: once upon a time, I was a young girl headed straight for an eating disorder.

It was summer, and I'll never forget the day or where I was: sitting on my parent's porch in Milwaukee enjoying some QT with Nana. This was the summer I'd gotten a little chunky. Well, OK, I guess I was always a little chunky. But Nana didn't put it quite so delicately. "You're fat, Susie," said she, as summer quickly turned to a different season altogether, "and you should eat yogurt."

With that, Nana unceremoniously shoved a tablespoon of yogurt into my mouth … uninvited. To this day, I cannot stand the sight—let alone the taste—of yogurt.

Why is this a case of classical conditioning? Well, let's recap: I learned to associate one thing with another; in this case, I associated eating yogurt with being fat. A neutral stimulus (yogurt) produced in me a strong emotion (hurt feelings from being called fat) just before yogurt was jammed down my impressionable windpipe.

Jaws had scary music to evoke dark emotions.

I had yogurt.

The result is the same: I was conditioned (I learned) to hate yogurt because once upon a time the feeling of shame, guilt, embarrassment, and worthlessness was so great that it forever created in me a negative response to a formerly innocent food.

Can you see the relationship now? Do you see how strongly our childhood process of socialization—play with dolls, wear a dress, don't get fat—forever affects our development as mature, capable, modern, intelligent adults? Can you see now how it's not the weight that upsets us, but the negative connotations connected with the weight?

If everyone from your granny to your mommy to your teacher to your best friends didn't associate "bad" with "fat," chances are weight would be a non-issue for thousands or hundreds of thousands of people suffering from EDs each year.

Classical conditioning—learning to associate a stimulus that is initially totally neutral or otherwise just plain ordinary or harmless (creepy music, a ringing bell, yogurt) with a specific response (fear, salivation, shame)—is at the root of my ED, your ED, every single one of my patients' EDs, and the body image and weight-specific hang-ups of most of your family, friends, acquaintances, and peers.

And that's just the beginning of the story ...

Operant conditioning: or, call in the reinforcements!

The story continues with another behavioral theory known as operant conditioning. Again, big word, simple concept. It goes kind of like this: we behave a certain way as a result of how our behavior is greeted by the world at large. If the result of our behavior is pleasant, we will most likely want to repeat that behavior. If the result is unpleasant, we won't want to do it quite so much.

For instance, a psychologist named B. F. Skinner wanted to test the results of reinforcement and punishment by observing rats in a laboratory. These very special lab rats were in a cage appropriately called the "Skinner Box" where a lever held the key to untold treats. Each time the rats stepped on the lever (or, in other words, when the rats engaged in an unsolicited behavior) the consequence was a pleasant one: a pellet of food came out! Yay! The rats quickly learned that each time they stepped on the lever food came out. Their behavior (stepping on the lever) resulted in a pleasant outcome (getting food). Voilà, positive reinforcement.

Conversely, if the opposite of something pleasant had happened each time the rat pushed the lever, say an electric shock or loud noise, the rat would have learned not to engage in the behavior that elicited such an unpleasant consequence. (We call this "positive punishment," or the delivery of an unpleasant stimulus ... but no need to get too clinical here.)

Rats not your bag? Let's put it into more human terms: let's say that one night on the way home from work you decide to bring your boyfriend a surprise gift such as a new CD by that punk band he's been talking so much about lately. Thoughtful, right? Pleasant surprise, huh? Well, imagine that instead of repaying you with a peck on the cheek or a cooked meal, he slaps you in the face! Not too pleasant a reaction, huh?

But maybe he had a bad day; maybe the surprise CD reminded him of an old girlfriend who broke his heart (classical conditioning, right?) so you try again the next night. Same thing happens: wham, slap in the face. But you're no quitter, so you give it the old college try and hope the third time's a charm.

Oh well, so sorry, smack; your boyfriend slaps your face the minute you hand over the sweet, surprise gift. By the way, after we try and try and try, only to always, constantly get unpleasant results, and we finally give up ... we call this Learned Helplessness. (You may want to remember this term for later on in the book.) The theory of "learned helplessness" was developed by Martin Seligman and S.F. Meir through experiments going back to 1965.

Now, what are the chances you'll ever bring your boyfriend a new CD again? Zero, right? That is operant conditioning in a nutshell; the consequence following your behavior, pleasant or unpleasant, strongly determines whether or not you'll engage in that behavior again. In short, an unpleasant consequence will result in the reduction of the behavior that resulted in the consequence.

Birth of a food sneak!

So, how did this operant conditioning stuff affect little me? Well, let me tell you! From the ripe old age of nine onward, my brother Jonny and I—Nana used to call us "the little couple"—flew to Syracuse every year, twice a year, to visit Nana. Remember good old Nana? Well, in typical holiday fashion, not long after we arrived we would sit down for dinner and start eating.

When Nana felt like I'd had enough—which was never even close to the same time as I thought I'd had enough—Nana would take my plate away and make me watch everyone else eat. At bed time, once Nana was asleep, I would beg Jonny to go to the fridge to get me some food. Dutifully, he would bring me Pinwheel cookies (the ones with chocolate on the outside and marshmallow on the inside with a yummy cookie crust) and I would literally devour them!

So, from age nine onward, I learned that I had to sneak food. I was praised for eating little in the presence of people—"My, what will power you have, little Susie!" I also felt comforted (pleasant consequences), when I stuffed my face with goodies when I was alone. And thus, before I had even turned 10, the endless binge cycle began.

Body double

Later, during college, Nana sent me to Chicago every few months to visit my uncle. (They must have been in cahoots together on this whole "get Susie skinny scheme.") Well, it just so happened that my uncle (Fred) was a make up artist and hair dresser for movie stars. (He lived in Chicago, worked in LA.)

Lest you think this was a small reprieve from the family pressures of the dinner table back home, being batted forth by Mom and Nana, well, it was no vacation. It was more like Beauty School Boot Camp!

Uncle Freddy would pick me up from the airport and immediately take me straight to clubs downtown in Chicago where we would party all night while he insisted on parading me around on his arm like the next porno queen. The next morning he would wake me up at the crack of dawn after about three or four hours of sleep and take me to his gym for a "super circuit" workout.

Once inside the gym, he would force me to exercise until I was physically exhausted and gagging on my own bile, while he pulled me up by my ponytail, forcing me to keep working out. He might as well have been classically trained in operant conditioning instead of make up and hair!

The thinner I became, the more *reinforcement* I got. He would dress me up in beautiful clothes and show me off on his arm. I adored my uncle and wanted to make him proud of me. So, I listened to him. I obeyed him. I *repeated* the behaviors that brought with them the *rewards/consequences* that were pleasant—his love.

It was no different than if I had brought him a special CD and he'd slapped me in the face. What got a pleasant reaction from him, I repeated (working out until exhaustion and nausea, looking pretty on his arm). What got a negative reaction from him, I stopped cold turkey (eating, resting).

If only I'd been as concerned with *my* emotions as much as I was *his* …

Then, one day, I got off the plane in Chicago, and he told me my face was "sunken in" and I looked "gray." I was immediately taken aback and felt terrible, like I had done something wrong. But I worked out, as directed. I starved, as promised. What more—what less—could I have done? In the same breath, he told me that if I would lose five more pounds (talk about sunken), he'd—get this—buy me fake boobs. (Yuck!)

Why in the world would I want to *add* more weight to my body? (Anorexics don't want to look like women! They want to keep their twelve-year-old boyish figures!) So maybe he didn't know as much about operant conditioning as I thought.

Gross! Yuck! I was so confused. He wanted me to lose *more* weight, but my face already looked grey and sunken in. He had always looked so proud to have me walk into a room on his arm, tight and svelte and dressed to the nines, but now he wanted me to have big fake breasts and look like a common street-walker?

Why couldn't anyone in my family simply accept me for who I was?

OK, so that's how I learned operant conditioning long before I ever studied it in Psych 101. So, let me give a quick recap: if the result of our behavior is pleasant, we will most likely want to repeat that behavior. If the result is unpleasant, we won't want to do it quite so much.

Back to Miami I went, more and more confused, and more and more alone in my own little messed up head. The isolation was difficult to swallow.

Despite the hordes of beautiful people swirling around the Miami sidewalks like hurricanes of confetti, there was still no one to hear me, no one to listen. It was my destiny to struggle through this period alone. No, not alone. Of course my "friend" ED came back with me, and together we shacked up for the duration.

If food is the drug, what is the high?

Now I want to give one last example to really drive home the theory of operant conditioning: If a drug addict loses his job—or his wife or his kids or his home or his teeth—because of his drug use, isn't that a pretty unpleasant consequence of his bad behavior? So, if that's unpleasant, why does he keep drinking and drugging? Sadly, the answer is because the initial, immediate response to that drug—the high—is more powerful (by far) than the secondary processes involved in finding a new job, moving out of his house, scrounging for his food, whatever.

Speaking of food, the feeling is quite similar: what those of us who have issues with food have in common with drug or alcohol addicts is that "high" we get. Again, the immediate gratification is what we are all craving. With anorexics, the high of starvation beats all of the other medical consequences of their very real, very dangerous disease. For the compulsive overeater and the bulimic, the food they gorge on while bingeing satisfies a need to escape the emotions that drive them to eat. For the bulimic, vomiting gives them a high and a release of all the painful emotions. Like all deep-seated psychological processes, the cycle is very difficult to break, but not impossible!

Social learning theory/modeling (It's not about super models!)

No discussion of ED would be complete without talking about models. And I know you've heard this before, but there's another element here I'd like to discuss. For starters, we all know that modeling is the extreme of extremes. Abigail Natenshon of EmpoweredParents.com, explains the sheer disproportion of "average women" to the models so many of us emulate: "Models twenty years ago weighed 8 percent less than the average woman. Today they weigh 23 percent less."

You may think that emulating models makes you feel powerful. The opposite is actually true: "A psychological study in 1995 found that three minutes spent looking at a fashion magazine caused 70 percent of women to feel depressed, guilty, and shameful," says Natenshon. The worst part is this: no one empowers supermodels to look any different, because what they do makes so many people so much money. They actually get rewarded for being unhealthily thin and, in the process, we who are susceptible to ED see their pictures and think, "Well, they're on the cover of a magazine; they must be doing something right." Right?

Wrong.

One more learning theory to go for now and, lucky you, it has its origins in the circus. (Well, kind of.) Bobo was a clown—a very special clown. He was a clown you could blow up and, thanks to a weight in his base, would stand up and allow you to punch him, time and time again, only to bounce right back up and be there, in your face, smiling like Bobo always smiled.

Well, Stanford psychologist Albert Bandura did a study using the Bobo doll. Dr. Bandura would put two children in separate rooms with a wall between them featuring a single pane of mirrored glass. On one side of the glass was a child encouraged to beat the crap out of a Bobo doll. Alone in the room, all he saw was his reflection as he pummeled poor Bobo. From time to time he would receive a reward for his efforts: candy, chocolate, cake, and the like.

On the other side of the mirror sat the second child, taking this all in, watching his peer pummel a blow-up doll and being rewarded for it. When it came time for the children to reverse roles, what do you think the second kid did? That's right: he beat Bobo up even harder than the first kid and got twice as many rewards.

This very simple experiment had massive repercussions in the psychiatric community. and with it as an inception, Dr. Bandura went on to perfect his "social learning theory." Basically, Bandura's social learning theory hypothesized that children learn from modeling the behaviors of others. Specifically, if they watch someone perform a specific behavior over and over, they would then "model" that behavior. They had learned it through social interaction: observing someone else do something socially acceptable over and over again.

In this case, the behavior was violent, but the violence was made acceptable in the experiment by the fact that the children who did the violence were so often rewarded for it. His verdict: We can learn through modeling behaviors.

Put your own experience with social learning theory (bet you never knew you'd done anything so scientific in your life, right?) to the test: have you ever watched someone perform a behavior, only to repeat it in your own life because they've given you the unconscious "OK" to do so?

Let's revisit our favorite ED setting: the family dinner table. If Mommy models small servings on her plate, that's what you'll do too, right? But if

Daddy makes a big joke of wolfing down his meal and expecting you to do the same, who will you model?

This confusing state of affairs will linger and, over time, present you with a conflict of interests: on one hand you know that less is better, but more tastes/ feels better. What to do? What to do? In many cases, this unpleasant parental modeling leaves you in a lifelong quandary where you know you should be modeling your mother but feel better modeling your father, so that the guilt piles up along with the pounds.

Now, there could be a healthy alternative. Eventually all children grow up; that's nature. And let's say one day you grow up to find yourself in the middle of Saturday afternoon modeling Mom and Dad watching TV in the living room instead of exploring the great outdoors. But it's a beautiful day, and you're restless, and God knows all three of you could use a little fresh air. So instead of modeling them watching TV, you could all model each other taking a hike, walking around the block, going out for a round of golf or even putt-putt. What I want to leave you with as we exit our section on behavioral theories is that your behaviors can be changed. Because your behaviors have been learned, they can be unlearned! They are reversible: you can turn the tides through positive action and personal accountability.

Why, just look at me!

ED prevention tips for parents, teachers and coaches: What you do is as important as what you don't!

In order to be better models to our children we must learn more about ourselves. Here are two simple lists regarding modeling behaviors that can help to prevent EDs in the future:

Do:

1. *Be the solution, not the problem.* Scrutinize your own attitudes and thoughts about weight and body image. Be honest, truthful, and forthcoming with yourself. Then consider how these feelings and prejudices might be communicated to your children in your attitudes (negativity about weight or size), comments (fat-centric words or phrases), or even non-verbal responses (like wincing at the sight of an obese stranger).

2. *Be a role model at the dinner table first, the fitting room second.* Do your best to encourage and "model" healthy eating by being sensible and moderate in all meals.

3. *Listen before speaking; then speak carefully.* Words spoken in haste to very sensitive individuals can hurt for years, and maybe a lifetime, while paying lip service to a child's real and apparent concerns is equally damning. Take seriously what your child is saying, feeling, and doing, not simply how they look.

4. *Move it or lose it.* Help your child to understand how great it feels to be active and to enjoy what their bodies can do for them. The more you model this behavior, the more apt they are to engage in it with you.

5. *Danger! Danger!* Discuss the dangers of overeating and under-eating.

6. *Self matters!* Do whatever you can to promote the self-esteem and self-respect of your children in intellectual, athletic, and social endeavors.

7. *Let censorship take a backseat to common sense.* Make a commitment to help children understand and resist ways in which television, magazines, and other media distort the true diversity of human body types. Don't imply that a slender body means power, excitement, and sexuality.

8. *Open up an honest, inviting dialogue.* Talk about different body types and how they can all be accepted and appreciated.

9. *Learn how moderate exercising promotes stamina and cardiovascular fitness.* The goal is to use exercise as a path to better health, not a quick trip to slim down, tighten up, get buff, or become beautiful.

10. *Educate yourself before teaching your child.* Learn about the dangers of trying to alter one's body shape through dieting.

11. *Knowledge is power; power is control.* Learn about the importance of eating a variety of foods in well-balanced meals and snacks consumed at least six times a day. Speak with your nutritionist. Don't just fall for the hype and hyperbole of slick packaging or fad diets.

12. *Equal opportunities bring more opportunities … for all.* Give boys and girls similar opportunities and encouragement.

13. *Love your child unconditionally no matter their shape, size, or weight.* Their body shape does not define them any more than does their hair, eye, or lip gloss color. Love starts from the inside out, not the other way around.

Don't:

1. *Don't label types of food as the good guys or the bad guys.* Avoid labeling foods as "safe," "good," "bad," "dangerous," or "fattening." These terms are relative and misleading. This only further empowers food to an unrealistic status.

2. *Don't comment on weight or body types (yours, your child's, or anyone else's).* Insults, stereotypes, or labels about weight or body types often slip out because they are one of our last "acceptable prejudices."

3. *Don't diet or encourage your child to diet.* Diets do more harm than good. If you are trying to lose weight, do so on your own, and don't make your child an observer or participant.

4. *Don't set parameters like "finish what's on your plate" or "you've had enough."* Allow your child to determine when he or she is full.

5. *Don't use food as a prize or a penalty.* Food is neither a reward nor punishment. Don't use it as such.

6. *Don't make negative comments while weighing your child.* As we've seen with classic conditioning, the scale will become the bell to Pavlov's dogs, and send your child scurrying for food to appease the emotional scars of painful weigh-ins. As a matter of fact, I suggest letting your child's doctor or dietician weigh your child, taking that responsibility out of your hands altogether. This allows the family to keep their parent-child relationship in tact.

7. *Don't foster a climate of tolerance for teasing, name-calling, blame-gaming or ridicule.* Don't let siblings, friends, neighbors, or other adults call your child names, even if they're so-called "harmless" like "chubs" or "tubby." Teasing, like this is not cute, and does more harm than it will ever do good. Allowing one family member to be the butt of jokes taints the entire family.

8. *Don't limit your child's caloric intake unless a physician requests that you do this because of medical problems.* Calorie deprivation is not the answer to weight loss nor a better life.

9. *Don't make body shape, beauty, weight, or size an issue.* Instead, model healthy behavior. Lead by example with health as the goal, not unattainable beauty.

10. *Don't avoid activities simply because they call attention to your child's weight and shape (swimming, sunbathing, dancing, etc.).* The family that plays together, stays together.

11. *Don't imply that girls are inferior to boys.* For instance, boys should do as much or as little housework as girls, girls should be encouraged to play the same games as boys, and vice versa.

12. *Don't use weight as a condition for love.* Such as, "I'd love you even more if you lost a few pounds" or "My love would grow if your waist size would shrink." Such messages can inflict as much damage, if not more, than a punch to the gut!

A well-rounded self and solid self-esteem are perhaps the best antidotes to mindless dieting and disordered eating, which we all know to be at the heart of our various EDs.

What it all means for you!

Phew! You made it through my mini-version of Psych 101, and all without having to take out a #2 pencil! I hope you're still with me, and understand now more than ever how psychology plays a much bigger role in your eating disorder than does a scale, mirror, tape measure, or seamstress.

Your ED is not about the weight. It simply isn't. That is why, in a book about body image and weight issues, I spent the very first chapter crunching difficult, sophisticated, and challenging psychological theories into bite-size nuggets so that you could swallow them whole and feel good knowing that, at long last, you are swallowing the truth!

You are a victim, plain and simple. I was a victim. We are victims of society's roles: for boys, for girls, for mothers, for daughters, for fathers, for sons, for teachers, and for students. We have been taught, time and time again, year in and year out, that food is good, but fat is bad, and where has that left us? Socialized to the point of extinction and more confused about our own eating habits than ever.

We are victims of classical conditioning. We learned at a young age that the dinner bell meant chow time, that the spinning reels of a movie meant popcorn, soda, and candy, and that the ice cream churn meant a cold treat on a hot summer night. We learned from the very beginning that food makes us happy, and as a result we've been unhappy about food ever since!

We are victims of operant conditioning. We learned to treat food as a drug. Much like a drug, we give foods, or food-related experiences, drug-related terms. We zone out in a "sugar coma" or bounce off the walls on a "sugar high." We get "brain freeze" from too much ice cream too fast and complain about, yet long for, the "nitrite effect" of our Thanksgiving turkey. Our food addictions are no less overpowering than drug or alcohol addictions, and no easier to treat.

We are victims of social learning theory. We have modeled those who didn't deserve modeling and ignored those who did. We have turned years of conflicting images, actions and messages into a lifetime of body image issues that are bordering on insanity.

In short, we are victims of ourselves. We have boxed ourselves into a way of life that is unhappy, unsatisfying, and, quite frankly, unlivable. We cannot sustain such idealistic weights, improper proportions, unhealthy eating habits, and unsavory regurgitation schedules without suffering massive, and in some cases irreversible damage, to our poor, sensitive bodies.

We are, quite literally, killing ourselves. Not to feel better, but to look better. Aren't you tired of being a victim? I know I am. I am tired of fighting every day to overcome something that was planted inside me that warm summer day when yogurt was shoved in my face and shame about my weight was shoved down my throat and my happiness, pride and sense of security were shoved under the carpet, never to be seen again for another twenty some years.

Two long decades of victimization, and I'm still not out of the woods! How about you? Can I help take you where no therapist has gone? Will you let me lead you out of the darkness and into the light? Can I be the one to make you see how pointless and painful being a victim can truly be?

We're not quite there yet; in fact, we've only just begun, but if you stick with me and trust me, I promise you that with each new chapter, with each new theory, lesson, or practice, you will be less of a victim and more of an independent spirit.

Eager and willing to be transformed, empowered, and ready to soar?

Then let's keep going!

Letters to ED, to our bodies, to ourselves:

Dear ED,

I wrote you a poem. I hope you hate it. I hope you love it. I hate you. I love you:

Lovely Bones

lovely bones
press against her
pale, cold skin.
two black eyes
show through all
the makeup.
her stomach
is loud,
calling out hunger.
she gets weaker
with every step,
occasionally
losing balance.
he's so very happy
as her smile fades away.
she had listened
to his words,
harsh and demanding.
it still wasn't
good enough;
she would never
be good enough
for him.
she was

near death

once again.

her heart was

skipping beats;

he was smiling.

"you did OK,"

he told her

as she slowly

faded away

with nothing

left to show

except her lovely bones.

Sincerely,

"Jasmine"

CHAPTER 3

Mission Possible—I Think, Therefore I Am

(Coping With Your Negative Self-talk ...)

OK, gang, still with me? I know we've touched on a lot of hardcore behavioral theories thus far, but I wouldn't be discussing them (let alone taking the time to write all this down) if it wasn't absolutely, positively, 100 percent vital for you to understand the central message I keep coming back to, which is this: It's not about *what you weigh*. Everything you've ever learned about food, weight, or your own self-worth is what's lurking under the surface.

Yes, it really is just that simple.

Of course, it's also just that complicated.

Like an iceberg, what lurks beneath the surface is about a hundred times bigger than the tip sticking out of the water and causing everyone to point at you (or so you think).

As anyone with an ED can tell you, losing weight is the easy part; just starve yourself, or exercise to physical exhaustion. It's what happens next that gives us the real trouble: dealing with the fact that we're so afraid of our bodies that we let them control us all day, every day and giving ourselves over to fears related to weight, food, body size, and shape. That's what's lurking under the surface, waiting to tear a hole in our bow and sink us so that we're all gone and all our thoughts of weight, shame, guilt, body size, insignificance, bingeing, starving, or purging are gone at last as well.

This chapter is going to help you get in touch with what's down there, hiding beneath the surface, dragging your emotions ever deeper into depression, fear, guilt, anxiety, and shame. In chapter four, we will be discussing how this negative, irrational, and self-destructive self-talk spirals into these strong negative emotional feelings and what we can do to counteract it. This chapter is about self-talk, and why the thoughts murmuring through your head constantly are at the heart of why your weight has so very little to do with your ED.

OK, so what exactly *is* self-talk? Is it really as simple as talking to yourself? (I wish; this book would be about fifty pages shorter if it were!) Well, for starters, self-talk is at the heart of a causal relationship. In other words, the thoughts that make up our self-talk result in behaviors. That is because *thoughts* and *behaviors* are interrelated. That means they do not stand exclusive of each other; to change one essentially means to change them both. But don't fret, this is actually good news!

Think of it this way: have you ever seen a garden hose with a bulge in it? What happens when you try to press the bulge down? It doesn't go away, right? It just moves somewhere else. Press down on a bulge at the front of the hose and it moves to the middle; press down on the middle and it moves to the back.

Your thoughts and behaviors are also interconnected. You can't press down on a certain thought and expect to stop thinking about it any more than you can will yourself to stop behaving in a certain way without really, truly understanding why the behavior needs to change in the first place.

So, no we can't simply suppress negative thinking and make it go away. For now, know this: it's like chasing that proverbial bulge in our mental garden hose; until you get to the root of the universal problem that's causing the bulge, the hose will never work right again.

Our thoughts can affect our behavior, and our behavior can affect our thoughts. So take heart; what made your thoughts and behaviors so damaging before—the fact that one elicited the other, and vice versa—makes them ripe for wellness now. Changing one will actually help you change the other! That's right; we can change our self-talk, and we can change our behaviors ... just like that!

What is self-talk?

Self-talk is more than just mumbling to yourself about why this skirt won't fit or that parking space won't open up. Self-talk is that constant, gurgling, ever present stream of consciousness that follows us everywhere we go throughout the day.

It's the mental list that pops into your head the minute you wake up, the minor irritations that announce themselves throughout our day. It's the incessant subconscious whispering that keeps us up at night tossing and turning.

Self-talk is perhaps a bit misleading; it's less about what we say and more about what we think. Talking aloud to ourselves is actually different from the self-talk I am discussing here in this chapter. We can control what we say out loud, and even what we answer. Don't believe me? Try this little test: next time you're in a crowded elevator or standing in a standing-room-only movie theater or dining in a restaurant jam-packed with a forty-five-minute wait, start talking to yourself. Out loud! Loud enough for all those other people to hear. Won't do it, will you? That's because talking to ourselves is a conscious act; we can control it, turn it on and off at will.

However, the thoughts that just pop into our heads at any given moment—those automatic thoughts—are unconscious (out of our immediate awareness) and totally out of our control. And, while we may not be able to control those intrusive little suckers from coming into our heads any time they feel like it, we *can* manage what we do with them once they've planted themselves. If we don't learn to control them, they will inevitably control us!

The self-talk that brings us down, lifts us up, and basically has us repeating thoughts that lead to behaviors all day long, every day, over and over again is a constant babbling mental stream of information, disinformation, misinformation, miscues, and mysteries that has baffled scientists as long as there's been science.

What can non-dairy creamer teach us about self-talk?

In trying to demystify self-talk for you I'll use a common example: let's say you wake up in the morning, cueing into the usual clutter that fills your head upon waking, only to lunge for the fridge halfway through your second cup of coffee and notice that you're almost out of non-dairy creamer. No need to make a list; that's what self-talk is for, right?

Throughout your day, you continually tell yourself that you must have that non-dairy creamer. On the way home, you head into the convenience store, are lured by all the come-ins and come-ons, and, on your way to the dairy cooler, forget all about your non-dairy creamer. Instead you emerge with a sack of two dozen things you'll never need in a million years.

Halfway home, your helpful self-talk reminds you about the non-dairy creamer!

Of course, we're talking about a little more than coffee creamer here. I mean, this is your life! And the self-talk we'll examine specifically, is that which drives your behavior, whether you know it or not. But take that non-dairy creamer and extrapolate it out. Non-dairy creamer can stand for anything we want: health, happiness, that new job, a new home, better health, or a longer life.

If we take the example of non-dairy creamer and apply it to self-talk, we'll see just how damaging it can be. For instance, let's say you forget the non-dairy creamer and, about halfway home, suddenly remember that you forgot it. Now the self-talk really kicks in:

> *"I can't believe you forgot the creamer. How stupid are you? You've been thinking about it all day, writing yourself little sticky notes. Bet you forgot those, too, huh? Gheez, you are really worthless, you know that? If you can't remember a little thing like non-dairy creamer, what can you remember? What a moron. No one will ever love you!"*

Suddenly, this self-talk, this damaging internal dialogue, becomes the spark that ignites harmful ED behavior. Now, because you forgot a $1 can of creamer you go home, binge and purge or starve yourself, repeat a vicious cycle, and do unknown damage to your already vulnerable body, all because the voices inside your head won't turn off until you do.

The danger of self-talk

That is the real danger of negative, destructive self-talk: it's insidious. It builds up in you, day after day, and flares up when least expected. Persons without an ED can see through their negligible self-talk to logically turn the car around, fish out a dollar and change, walk back into the store, buy the darn creamer, get back in their car, and drive home without starving themselves or bingeing and purging. Or they can simply wait until the morning and get the creamer then, and still have a pleasant evening at home without spending every waking moment calling themselves names and wondering what in the world is wrong with them!

Why? Is it because they're better than you? Stronger? Smarter? Hardly! They either don't have the level of negative self-talk that people with an ED do or, if they hear negativity in their self-talk, they have mastered ways to tackle, short circuit, or eliminate the negativity altogether.

It's *not* a matter of better or worse, stronger or weaker, smarter or dumber; it's merely a matter of learning to tune into your self-talk, recognize it for what it is, and then empower yourself to do something about it!

How often does our self-talk derail us rather than empower us? Non-dairy creamer, sure, but what about the bigger picture? Non-dairy creamer as … life? How often have we thought about going back to school, for instance, reminding ourselves all day long to zip by the local college campus and pick up a catalog when, lo and behold, our self-talk conveniently helps us forget, or, as is more common, "self-talks" us out of it?

How often have we self-talked ourselves out of going to the gym, or calling that guy from class who was interested in us, or reconnecting with our family, or trying out for that part in the school play, or looking into that job, or any number of other things we wanted to accomplish, only to shoot ourselves in the foot?

Much like that favorite classic from our childhood *The Little Engine That Could*, we'll be discussing the positive self-talk—*I think I can, I think I can, I think I can*—as well as the negative self-talk many of us experience, unfortunately, much more frequently—*I know I can't, I know I can't, I know I can't!*

Sounds pretty familiar, right? That's because self-talk goes deep, deep, *deep* into the psyche; it's like runoff from your very soul. And it's on a continuous loop that just runs through your brain all day long. The thoughts may seem disconnected, but if you pay attention, you will uncover a running theme.

Over the years, certain themes in our self-talk get repeated. Some of us can't commit to relationships, jobs, or even plan future goals. Some of us avoid confrontation. Some of us are prejudiced against certain religions, doctrines, races, or creeds. Some of us are afraid to try new things simply because we have *convinced* ourselves for so long that we *can't*.

All of these are common themes in our internal dialogue. The beauty of self-talk is that when it's empowering, we can be built up, made to feel confident, and actively participate in our own recovery. The danger is that, when left unchecked, our negative self-talk can fester, grow, and eat away at the life we so desperately desire.

Self-talk cuts deep over time

Self-talk is like the Colorado River, which eventually cut a swatch across Arizona to create a nearly mile deep gorge known as the Grand Canyon. Sure, it took a few million years, but that's the power of perseverance: it works!

Unfortunately, for many of us, self-talk wears down rather than builds up our confidence. We gradually get into a habit of "talking ourselves down" all the time, and eventually we actually start to believe our own bad press. Most of the time this starts in childhood, with us "mimicking" in our heads what others have told us out loud: we're not good enough, we're too slow, not smart enough, too fat, too thin, too tall, too short, or we'll never amount to anything.

Oftentimes we misconstrue what somebody says, and instead of asking them to clarify, we repeat the wrong version in our heads. Take the word "ignorant," for instance. Most of us immediately equate the word ignorant with stupid, but in fact it means something quite the opposite: you can have a PhD in rocket science but still be ignorant about changing the oil in your car. Ignorant doesn't mean stupid at all, it just means you haven't quite acquired that particular skill set yet, be it oil changing or brain surgery. Yet our self-talk takes the word and runs with it.

What does your self-talk sound like? Is it positive and encouraging? Does it nurture your ideas, give you the freedom to explore new opportunities, and embolden you to try new things? Or does it knock you down, tear away at your self-confidence, and repeatedly remind you how big, fat, dumb, and worthless you really are? (You really aren't.)

My goal for this chapter is to make sure that you recognize what self-talk is, how it works, where it came from, and, most importantly, how to actively change your self-talk so that it is more positive, more constructive, and more self-preserving! After all, what's all this theory if we can't put it into practice?

What drives self-talk? It starts here …

Psychoanalytic psychology: the genesis of talking

OK, gang. Here is where the rubber hits the road, so to speak. But we can't discuss self-talk without "talking" about the man who was there from the beginning. So please stick with me here; it's important.

You've come through so much on your journey to healing. I promise that if you just stay the course despite the words that might make you close another book—*psychoanalytic psychology*, for example—you will be rewarded with the lasting prize of lifelong healing.

So, here goes: a psychiatrist named Sigmund Freud (you might have heard of him) believed that mental life is like an iceberg: only a small part is exposed to view. This part is called the consciousness or our awareness. However, Freud believed that most psychological disorders originate from repressed (hidden) memories and instincts stored in the unconscious.

This is the area of the mind that lies below our personal awareness. According to Freud, our behavior is deeply influenced by unconscious thoughts, impulses, desires, memories, and other repressed material that has been lying dormant since childhood. Just as the enormous mass of iceberg below the surface destroyed the ocean liner *Titanic*, the unconscious may similarly damage our psychological lives.

Freud's psychodynamic theory proposes that we are largely a product of our unconscious. Our unconscious mind takes in all of the stimuli from our environment without any filter. It is directly sent as fact; there is no moral ambiguity, shades of gray, or wishy-washiness about it. The unconscious mind does not differentiate what is real or fake, true or false, fact or fiction, right or wrong, and good or bad. (Do you remember our "ignorant" versus "dumb" example?)

As a result, our thoughts and actions are a product of all that "junk" that's buried deep down inside; Just think how long you've been alive and how much of that emotional junk you've accumulated in your unconscious mind! Even if you're only a teenager, you've had more than enough time to carve out your own Grand Canyon of guilt, resentment, shame, and insecurity through no fault of your own.

Every put-down, slight, or offense. Every glance in the mirror, pair of pants that didn't fit, or Victoria's Secret commercial that made you feel like you could never measure up. Every breakfast, lunch or dinner. Every all-you-can-eat buffet or quick-fast diet drink. Every boyfriend or girlfriend who ever dumped you. Every test you ever failed, job you ever lost, or prom you never went to. It's all there, piled up high, waiting to undermine your smile every time you think of "turning that frown upside down."

The seeds of self-talk are the seeds of our design

How, you ask, does that make a difference in your life? Let the story begin: the words, memories, criticism, ideas, hurts, pains, and situations from our past and present, be they good, bad or indifferent, have all become a part of our psyches.

Our memories and past hurts don't just define us, they *design* us. We are hardwired by all that information and misinformation. Today yogurt disgusts me. My unconscious took the incident with my grandmother and the yogurt, shoved it deep, deep down in my psyche, and fed it back to me on a continual loop until this very day. My thoughts affect my behavior: I am repulsed when I see yogurt so I respond by not eating it.

If we haven't processed those things and learned to manage or cope with them effectively, they manifest themselves in some form of self-destructive behavior later in life.

For the purposes of my story, they manifested themselves into ED behaviors.

For the purposes of this chapter, we all manifest self-destructive self-talk.

Of course, later on during my healing phase I did end up processing the now infamous "yogurt incident" because I can now understand it all and apply 'my tools' to overcome everything, as I counsel my patients.

Just think: I'm forty-three years old, and I recall an incident so many years back. It must have been significant. How many disturbing events do *you* recall that clearly? I bet you recall many yourself. It's truly sad how these things latch onto our psyches, huh? How powerful these messages can be!

OK, so you made it through the condensed version of the lecture about the unconscious and the importance of talk therapy. I'm sure we'll be revisiting this topic and Freud again throughout this book. Thanks for your patience. Now, it's back to self-talk and how it affects you.

Every conscious moment of our lives is filled with self-talk; it is our ongoing, internal language. Self-talk includes all of the sentences with which we view and interpret the world. The problem arises when our self-talk is faulty or irrational.

If our internal dialogue is faulty, we experience stress and emotional difficulties that take the form of depression, anxiety, rage, guilt, and a sense of worthlessness. Changing our self-talk is very difficult; it has run so deep for so long that you might as well try changing the course of a river or turning back an avalanche. But try we must, for if we are ever to truly heal we must attack our ED at its source, and that is our psyche (our unconscious) not our stomach or our weight!

When we have ideas about the way we *should* be, we tend to find ourselves feeling bad and worthless when we fail to live up to those standards. But, in reality, the *standard* is bad because that is what is irrational. Hence, much of what we feel is caused by what we tell ourselves, and the ways in which we *choose* to interpret situations.

The worst part is that, left to our own devices from a very young age, we might have come out all right. Just imagine how good you'd feel about food if someone, some event, or some thing in your formative years hadn't gone and ruined it for you. Just imagine how good you'd feel about what you see in the mirror if you didn't have glossy pictures of rail thin models cut out from the latest fashion mags and pasted around the mirror's borders.

Just think how much I'd love yogurt if Nana hadn't shoved it down my throat while telling me how fat and unattractive I was!

The power of positivity: an equation for uplifting thought

> *Situation* begets *perception* begets *interpretation (self-talk)* begets *emotion* begets *behavior.*

Positive self-statements are important to us in all aspects of our daily lives. They manifest themselves in any situation at all times. In 1961 Albert Ellis mentioned that (I paraphrase), "… our emotions have nothing to do with actual events."

And yet think of how much value (emotive response) we place on things (actual events). A watch is just a watch, unless it's a Rolex, which we "think" is better than a Timex. A car is just a car, unless it's a Mercedes, which we "think" is better than a Hyundai. (And, even according to Freud, sometimes a cigar is just a cigar is just a cigar!)

And weight? Well, logically, weight is a mere number. And yet there's very little logic applied to the issue of weight in this country. Why, just look how much emotion we place on the event of determining that number by stepping on a scale. What gets lost in translation from the event to the emotion? In between the event and the emotion is realistic or unrealistic self-talk.

It is this self-talk that produces the *emotions*. It is this self-talk that creates anxiety, anger, and depression. Ellis contends that the following is how our thoughts influence our emotions: Situation—perception—interpretation (self-talk)—emotions—behavior.

Sounds complicated, but we do it several thousand times a day. Let's apply the formula to a real-life event, say, shopping for our summer bathing suit. (Arrgh, I can already hear you flipping past this page!) Well, in our scenario, we are faced with a *situation*: summer is here and our old bathing suit is about ready to kick the bucket. The elastic's shot, the color's faded, it can barely keep its shape, and look at all those cute little bathing suits on display at the front of the department store!

Immediately our situation of buying a bathing suit creates a *perception*: this is going to suck! Now, on a purely physical level, buying a bathing suit is a relatively simple affair: grab your wallet, drive to the store, walk in the store, pick your favorite bathing suit, pay for the bathing suit, get in the car, drive home, put on the bathing suit, go to the beach, and live fabulously.

On an emotional level, however, we have years and years of baggage and unhealthy self-talk to help shade the experience (color our perceptions) for us. How fun do you think it was for me to go shopping for bathing suits with Nana?

How about you? Who was there in the dressing room with you, pointing out every flaw? Whomever it was, your unconscious mind stored the experience for you, helpfully repeating it back to you so that now your perception is all but cast in concrete: *this is going to suck!*

So, we have discussed two terms: situation and perception. What's left? We have three to go: interpretation (self-talk), emotions, and behavior. Let's go on, shall we? So, as we stand there next to the bathing suit aisle, gazing upon an assortment of colors, fabrics, shapes, stripes, polka-dots, and sizes, we have an ongoing *interpretation* in which our self-talk fuels a mini-panic attack of epic proportions.

Let's listen in, shall we? "Susie, come on. Put that back. You could never fit into that tiny thing; and, if you did you'd look ridiculous. Other girls could pull it off, sure. Smarter girls, prettier girls, tanner girls, taller girls, thinner girls, but you? Oh, dear, please. Look, here, the one with the aqua blue skirt and matching polka-dot swim cap. That's much more your speed …"

Sound familiar? What's next on our little shopping list of horrors? That's right: *emotions*. That's an easy one. How do you *feel* when you've had enough self-talk and walked out of the store carrying one bikini you know you'll never wear, one full-piece in the size you want to be, and the same exact full-piece in a size that fits? A better question than "how do you feel" might be "what don't you feel?" The list of emotions that result from the experience are as many and varied as the size, shape, cut, and fit of the bathing suits that created the emotions in the first place!

Best to move onto our last piece of the equation: *behavior*. We've already run the gamut from situation (buying our summer bathing suit) to perception (hating the thought of buying our summer bathing suit) to interpretation/self-talk (telling ourselves how bad we look in every single bathing suit) to emotions (feeling horrible, shamed, guilty, worthless, disgusting, depressed, or suicidal), now it's time to talk about behavior.

What do we do—physically, actively, specifically—when faced with this situation? How do we act? What specific actions do we carry out as a result of facing this particular situation? Well, for starters, we bought more than one suit. We spent too much. We blushed and stumbled our way from front door to bikini aisle to fitting room back to car.

We snapped at anyone who crossed our path and no doubt drowned our sorrows by partaking in our ED of choice the minute we got home. Yep, I went home to binge, purge, and start the vicious cycle all over again … after every single shopping spree with Nana! I just wanted to be thin for her! That's all I wanted. I wanted her to love me!

All of this is to explain that Albert Ellis was right after all: Situation begets perception begets interpretation (self-talk) begets emotion begets behavior.

The origin of negative self-talk

You may ask yourself, where does negative self-talk come from? In most cases, it is possible to trace negative thinking back to deeper-lying beliefs, attitudes, or assumptions about ourselves, others, and life in general. These basic assumptions have been variously called "scripts," "core beliefs," "life decisions," or "mistaken beliefs."

When it comes to self-talk, there is usually no shortage of teachers along the way! While growing up, we heard a variety of negative words and ideas from our parents, teachers, and peers, as well as from the larger society around us.

The resulting beliefs are typically so basic to our thinking and feeling that we do not recognize them as beliefs at all. We simply take them for granted as the true nature of reality: I am a bad person. Yogurt is the devil spawn. Bathing-suit shopping is torture. Every woman on the planet is prettier than me. No man will ever love me. I will never amount to anything. *Fill in your self-talk oriented belief here.*

Mistaken beliefs are at the root of much of the anxiety and depression we experience when grappling with our EDs. As we have seen, these mistaken beliefs are just that: we have taken an isolated incident, comment, put down, phrase, food group, or shopping experience and through negative self-talk and an unyielding, un-empathetic unconsciousness turned it into an epic drama of massive proportions. Be it looking in the mirror, raising a fork to our lips, sucking on a yogurt pop, or slipping into a trunk-ini, we have been paralyzed by the most mistaken of beliefs.

We are neither entirely guilty nor entirely without blame. Something slipped that initial thought into our head. It might have been a word (fat, jolly, skinny, hot, oaf, husky, model, cute). a phrase (take some weight off your mind, you'd be so much prettier if you lost five pounds, do fries come with that shake), an incident (changing in the girls' locker room for the first time, someone shoving yogurt down your throat, someone else yanking your dinner plate away), a meal (Thanksgiving, a boyfriend ordering salad for you on a date, a reduced fat, fat-free, or organic birthday cake the year you turned thirteen), or a person (mother, teacher, girlfriend, cheerleader), but at some point we stepped in with our own harmful self-talk and ran with it to create thoughts that directly resulted in behaviors. Underlying our anxious and depressive patterns of self-talk are basic destructive assumptions about ourselves and the way life is.

Repeat after me: negative thoughts lead to self-destructive behaviors

When we think or speak negatively, we will inevitably act (and feel) in ways that are congruent with these negative beliefs. Those negative *thoughts* will inevitably lead to self-destructive *behaviors*.

I repeat: *negative thoughts lead to self-destructive behaviors.*

Say it with me: *negative thoughts lead to self-destructive behaviors.*

Now, hear me out: this is more than mere "your attitude determines your altitude," bumper sticker stuff. We are talking about more than "I think I can, I know I can." You can't just read a positive affirmation on an inspirational poster and undo years and years of deeply ingrained negative self-talk and long-standing habitual self-destructive behaviors. This is proven, hardcore, cognitive-behavioral theory. It is the subject of research studies and dozens upon dozens of books.

We must learn to counteract the negative self-talk by literally thinking differently. You will never be able to silence self-talk, but you can definitely reprogram what your self-talk says so that you live a life free of unnecessary doubt and struggle.

Clearly, to overcome our EDs we must learn to *re-think* so we can learn to *re-behave*. We must stop beating ourselves up, mentally and physically, for what we perceive to be the truth when, in fact, reality is very much the opposite. One way we can do this is to learn a little more about something called Rational Emotive Behavior Therapy, or REBT:

Rational emotive behavior therapy, or REBT

Yeah, big words, I know, but we're not going to rewrite my old *Psych 101* textbooks here, so breathe easy. The most basic premise of Rational Emotive Behavior Therapy, or REBT, is that *almost all human emotions and behaviors are the result of what we assume, believe, or think* (about ourselves, about other people, and about the world in general). It is what we believe about the situations we face—not the situations themselves—that determines how we think and behave.

Back to my yogurt story. It exemplifies what Ellis says about thoughts versus behavior, in general, and Rational Emotive Behavior Therapy, in particular. The theory of REBT explains the way I behave when it comes to yogurt: avoiding it like the plague, taking pains to eat anything but yogurt, and avoiding the yogurt aisle in the grocery store. These are active, physical, observable behaviors based not on the physical properties of yogurt itself (which have been proven to be fairly healthful and positive for millions of people), but on my thoughts and my perceptions as they pertain to yogurt.

I believe that yogurt is bad and so my reality is that yogurt is bad. My perception defines my reality, regardless of what is really "real" or not. It's patently irrational, of course, and I'm a licensed, trained therapist, for goodness sake, and yet I was powerless to stop myself from engaging in this irrational behavior until I untrained myself.

Turning theory into action

The theories I present in this book are all well and good but we need to apply them to our present situations, or they could wind up as relatively useless information. As you might have already guessed, the theory of REBT assumes that these perceptions, these thoughts, are deeply, deeply rooted in our self-talk.

As we have seen, changing our deepest, darkest thoughts is daunting, which begs the question:

Is true change really possible?
(And, if so, how much can we really change?)

Let's talk about change for a minute. Now, for the purposes of our discussion, there are big changes and little changes. Little changes occur most often; they occur all the time, as a matter of fact. Of course, we don't accomplish big changes without the little ones being in place first. As we've all heard before, we can't walk until we crawl, right?

No, first we must take little steps, wobbly ones, on legs both uncertain and weak. Then, as we derive our strength from a renewed sense of experience and confidence, we take bigger steps, stronger steps, until at last we are not just walking, but running. In short, the little changes are what *make* the big changes. After all, you don't start at the top; the baby steps are what lead to the big goals.

To actually live healthier—to achieve fundamental and lasting change that has a direct impact on your ongoing recovery—involves modifying the underlying core beliefs that create such negative thoughts in the first place. In other words, to boil it down, serve it up, and make the leap from little change to *big* change: what we think determines how we behave. So, let's get rational (after I teach you what it's like to be irrational … but some of you already know that!)

Irrational thinking

1.   Prevents us from reaching our goals;

2.   Manufactures emotions that are both extreme and depressing;

3.   May lead to harmful behaviours;

4.   Distorts reality;

5.   Makes us misinterpret what is really happening;

6.   Makes logic a thing of the past.

Certainly, to change how we think can be considered *big* change. For those big changes, and even a few of the small ones, you occasionally need help, perhaps outside help.

Help is *out there*, gang!

In the meantime, we've got plenty of help *in here* …

How I learned to listen to my self-talk (and what you can learn from me!)

How do I know so much about negative self-talk? Well, besides the twenty-seven years of schooling and training it took to earn my wall full of fancy credentials, I got to know self-talk only too well on a personal basis. In fact, even to this day, my self-talk can be very, very negative if I'm not ever vigilant about analyzing it, reframing it, and eventually reversing it before it is able to attach itself to my now healthy psyche.

The following so-called "innocent" remarks made by my very own doctors, friends, family, and even absolute strangers eventually became comments that I internalized all of my life. And, since they became a part of my psyche (according to Freud), I started to adopt those comments as my very own self-talk. Eventually, I began to act out on them, as you will see:

Then:
(How I grew up to internalize all of the criticism)

- **Nana (when clothes shopping)** "Of course you look fat in that; you are fat."

- **Self-talk:** "I am fat. I am worthless. I will never look good in clothes."

- **Mom:** "Well, those are the kinds of girls that the boys want to show off. But you're the kind of a girl that the boys will want to marry one day."

- **Self-talk:** "I'm fat and ugly, and I am an embarrassment to be seen with."

- **Parents' friends:** "Your face is so pretty, too bad you can't just lose a little weight."

- **Self-talk:** "My weight is my worth."

- **Nana:** "You'll never find a husband if you don't lose some weight."

- **Self-talk:** "Men will never find me attractive. I'll never be married."

- **Nana:** "You'll never be successful if you're fat."

- **Self-talk:** "I will always be worthless. I will never amount to anything."

- **Overheard at party:** "She has such an awesome personality."

- **Self-talk:** "I am fat."

- **Doctor #2:** "She's always going to be average."

- **Self-talk:** "I will always be a loser."

- **Doctor #5** (you haven't even heard about this doctor yet): "You will always be heavy, because you are protecting yourself from pain."

- **Self-talk:** "I'll always be fat. I'll just keep eating."

What you believe … determines what you perceive: irrational beliefs and the ammunition to Stop Them!

In general, we all tend to have a core belief system: what is right, what is wrong, our preference for this, or our dislike of that. It is largely what makes us unique as individuals and allows us to have scruples to behave in polite society.

However, individuals with eating disorders have an uncommonly deeply ingrained core belief system. You might say that while most people have core belief systems, we have systems of dogma that literally dominate our thought patterns to the point of distraction, disruption, and destructiveness that manifests itself in dangerous behavior and poor health.

As a therapist, this deeply-ingrained, irrational belief system tends to be one of the most challenging of all variables for me to help my patients change. However, I have good news for my patients and for you: although change is tough, it's absolutely possible! I'm living proof!

I see change every day; it happens. The best part about big change is that it happens in small doses. It's kind of like the snowball that rolls downhill to become this huge spinning globe of ice and snow, or the mighty oak that grows from the tiny acorn, or the gigantic beanstalk that grows out of the … well, you get the point. Choose your simile, but just know that metamorphosis happens, all in each individual's due time. And, it cannot be forced … just gently guided.

Now, since this chapter is all about self-talk—in particular, changing negative self-talk to positive self-talk—I'm going to arm you with a few surefire "spins" to physically help you throw your self-talk a curve ball.

The following are some very common irrational beliefs that folks with EDs typically have; I deal with these in my office on a daily basis. Right below these irrational beliefs, I have written a sample of the rebuttal statements that I would teach my patients to use in order to practice refuting these self-destructive ED statements.

I don't really believe in scripts; I think that how we respond to situations, incidents, and statements must come from deep within, instinctually, and you can't memorize what you *should* say or *should* do.

However, as a start, I hope that you can at least see how the positive statements are clearly more rational than the negative ones. If I achieve this goal and this goal alone of stripping irrationality from your belief system, I will have truly accomplished what I set out to do by debunking negative self-talk in this chapter.

Please keep in mind that each individual is unique and each statement should be hand crafted to fit your individual needs. For now, feel free to use these statements as a template for your own attempts at fostering more positivity in your self-talk.

Notice too, how the positive statements are in present tense. Change is ongoing; it may have happened in the past, but unless it is going on *right now*, today, it simply isn't going to achieve its desired goal of lasting, permanent change. So be sure to respond to negativity in the present tense; it's a sure way to make doubtful self-talk a thing of the past.

Irrational self-talk versus positive self-statements

- **Irrational self-talk:** I need love and approval from those significant to me, and I must avoid disapproval from any source.

- **Positive self-statement:** Being loved and approved of by others is nice but not necessary for me to love myself.

- **Irrational self-talk:** To be worthwhile as a person I must achieve and succeed at whatever I do and make no mistakes.

- **Positive self-statement:** I am human, and I have the right to make mistakes.

- **Irrational self-talk:** My unhappiness is caused by things that are outside my control, so there is little I can do to feel any better.
- **Positive self-statement:** I have control over my thoughts and behaviors.

- **Irrational self-talk:** Because they are too much to bear, I must avoid life's difficulties, unpleasantness, and responsibilities.
- **Positive self-statement:** I am managing all obstacles that come my way.

- **Irrational self-talk:** Everyone needs to depend on someone stronger than themselves.
- **Positive self-statement:** I am self-sufficient. I am depending on myself.

- **Irrational self-talk:** Events in my past are the cause of my problems, and they continue to influence my feelings and behaviors now.
- **Positive self-statement:** The past is the past, and I am making a new beginning. I am the creator of my destiny.

- **Irrational self-talk:** Being overweight is the worst thing that can happen to me. If I am overweight, I'm a complete failure in the eyes of the world.
- **Positive self-statement:** I am worth more than my weight. I am beautiful both inside and out.

- **Irrational self-talk:** There are "good" and "bad" foods. Eating "bad" foods makes me a bad person. Eating "good" foods makes me a good person.
- **Positive self-statement:** I am a good person no matter what foods I choose to consume. There are no good or bad foods.

- **Irrational self-talk:** I must have total control over my actions in order to feel safe. Self-control is a sign of strength and discipline.
- **Positive self-statement:** As I make healthy *choices* I am powerful.

- **Irrational self-talk:** I must keep others happy no matter what the cost to me. I have to earn the love of others because I am an inferior person.
- **Positive self-statement:** I am responsible only for my happiness. I am worthy of others' love just the way I am.

- **Irrational self-talk:** External validation is the only way to measure my worth: calories, weight, grades, clothing size, etc.
- **Positive self-statement:** Internal validation is the key to my inner peace.

- **Irrational self-talk:** As soon as I _____, I will be able to give up _____ (fill in your ED).
- **Positive self-statement:** Life is happening now. I love myself unconditionally now.

- **Irrational self-talk:** I must be perfectly thin to be happy and successful.
- **Positive self-statement:** I am worthy as I am no matter what my size or weight.

- **Irrational self-talk:** Fat is horrible.
- **Positive self-statement:** I am beautiful from the inside out.

- **Irrational self-talk:** People will love me if I am thin.

- **Positive self-statement:** I love *myself* unconditionally. It is not my weight that determines my worth.

- **Irrational self-talk:** I have total control by not eating.
- **Positive self-statement:** I am more powerful as I engage in healthy behaviors.

- **Irrational self-talk:** Starving punishes those around me who have made me miserable.
- **Positive self-statement:** My mind and body deserve to be nourished. I am only punishing myself when I starve.

- **Irrational self-talk:** If I eat at all, I will never be able to stop.
- **Positive self-statement:** I am choosing to stop eating when my body feels full. My mind and body deserve to be nourished.

- **Irrational self-talk:** Other people who are strong can stop, but not me.
- **Positive self-statement:** I am a strong person, and I am making healthy choices for my mind and body.

- **Irrational self-talk:** Since I haven't succeeded yet, it proves that I just can't.
- **Positive self-statement:** I am succeeding today and always. The past is the past. Today is a new day.

- **Irrational self-talk:** Self-control is just too hard.
- **Positive self-statement:** I believe in my ability to succeed.

- **Irrational self-talk:** I deserve to have it easier. It's too hard.
- **Positive self-statement:** I am worthwhile enough to fight for what I want.

- **Irrational self-talk:** It's awful being deprived. I can't stand it!
- **Positive self-statement:** I am *choosing* to eat in moderation.

- **Irrational self-talk:** It's my nature to eat and eat. I was born this way.
- **Positive self-statement:** I am changing my habits today.

- **Irrational self-talk:** I need immediate gratification.
- **Positive self-statement:** I am capable of delaying gratification. I am learning to accept change.

- **Irrational self-talk:** Life is too boring without my favorite foods. So, I have to keep eating them.
- **Positive self-statement:** I am choosing to eat in moderation. I am finding other stimulating activities.

- **Irrational self-talk:** When they find an easier way to lose weight, I'll do it.
- **Positive self-statement:** I am worthy enough to make the effort to help myself today.

- **Irrational self-talk:** My therapist should make me stop; that's what I pay her for.
- **Positive self-statement:** I am succeeding with guidance from others.

- **Irrational self-talk:** Why should I stop eating my favorite foods if you don't have to?

- **Positive self-statement:** I am making healthier choices for *my* mind and body.

Warning: the ravages of abuse

One theory that some individuals who may have been sexually abused as children subscribe to is that they use their weight as a protection against repeated abuse. This has been a long time theory and one that permeates the minds of those who eat to, "stay safe."

"I need my weight so no one will find me desirable. This way no one can hurt me again." This is a statement commonly heard from those who have a tendency toward compulsive overeating. Whereas, interestingly, anorexics may feel the same way, by wanting to look like an underdeveloped girl (as opposed to a woman) because, "If I look like a woman, the men will hit on me and I will get hurt." In either of these cases, they engage in self-destructive behaviors so nobody else can destroy them ... *again*. Here, these individuals perceive a false sense of security. Meanwhile, ED is loving every minute of it. ED wins ... again! This time he's tricked you into thinking that he can slip in as comfort when, in fact, he's anything but. Keep in mind, ED isn't just ED; he's all of that "junk" lurking under the surface. In this case, that old abuse and the weight that makes no rhyme or reason to keep on or off.

I'd just like to mention that keeping the weight on or off will not protect you. You have to learn to cope with protecting yourself from the inside-out in order to combat relational pains. You and your therapist can work on those skills together.

Oh, and guess what? Remember I said that there had never been a Doctor #5 ... well, not for a while? There was eventually! And, guess what Doctor #5 told me? He said that I would always be fat, because it was my way to protect myself from being hurt! Yes he did. Can you believe it? Not exactly the best thing to tell someone who is prone to an eating disorder, huh?

So for years I figured, once again, that Doc #5 was right! ED agreed and told me to just keep eating: "Feed your face!" This sent me mouth-first into an eating frenzy. But, no, Sally needed me to be skinny to find a man and to be worth something and Freddy expected me to be perfect so I could look like his porno models, and ... oh no, what am I going to do? Confusion resulted. So, I figured

I'd eat, barf, and, well, you get the point! Until, I realized that I had a choice. We'll get to that in the next chapter! (Thank goodness, there's a way out!)

Before we close our discussion of self-talk though, I want to delve into something every person with ED confronts. (Oh, and everyone else on the planet deals with too):

Cognitive distortions: a list of the most common (and what you can do about them)

Why is so much of our self-talk negative? Think of it as mental sludge, and over the years this sludge builds up until it's the only thing our engines will run on.

We often think of habits as something we do: washing our hands too much, driving angry, saying "uhhm" before every new thought, smoking, interrupting people during conversations, or not responding to email promptly enough. But thoughts can be bad habits, too. That's what cognitive distortions are: bad habits of thought.

It is important to remember that cognitive distortions are not beliefs; they may be based on unrealistic beliefs, but the distortions are not beliefs themselves. Cognitive distortions are habits of thinking that can get you in trouble.

Distorted thinking styles are hard to diagnose and treat because they are bound up tightly with our way of perceiving reality. Even the most rational person on earth operates at some distance from reality. It is unavoidable, given the built-in programming of the human mind and senses; there is just too much emotional baggage along for the ride to do otherwise.

The word "distort" is such a powerful one, and it perfectly fits the description of this behavioral theory. If we think of "cognition" as *thought*, and "distortion" as *bent*, we can literally translate this phrase into human speak as "bent thoughts." And that's exactly what they are: thoughts that are bent, irrational thinking that does not develop in a straight line, as does rational thought, but that instead winds and twists and turns like a snake, eating away at our self-confidence and destroying our potential for good health.

So how do we break these bad habits of thought? How do we overcome cognitive distortions so that we can begin to renew the cycle of change within ourselves and reverse negative self-talk into positive self-talk? How do we straighten out these "bent thoughts?"

As they say in school, knowledge is power. Well, knowledge is power when you can apply that knowledge. If you can't apply it, then you're stuck with zip, zilch, nada, if you ask me … Oh, you didn't ask me, did you?

By recognizing the most common forms of cognitive distortion, we can at least begin to identify, and eventually change, them. Below you will find a quick discussion of each form of cognitive distortion, followed by a short list of how to counteract them. I hope you will find this newfound sense of knowledge to be applicable so you, too, can be truly powerful.

Overgeneralization:

Overgeneralization occurs when you take one fact or event (getting stood up; not being promoted), and make a general rule out of it (everybody hates me; I'm a failure), without testing the rule. For instance, you buy a bathing suit in a hurry and get home only to find out that it makes you look horrible, and as a result, you think that every bathing suit you ever buy from this day forward will always make you look horrible.

By the same token, let's say that you go out on a date with an artist-type who never calls you back after he drops you off at your doorstep. Overgeneralization: "All artist-types hate me!" Further overgeneralization: "Wait, the artist type was a *man*, so … *all* men must hate me, too!"

Both reactions set you up for just one thing: acting out in ways that lead to eventual destructive eating behaviors. What was lost in both scenarios? Power. You felt powerless when trying on a bikini and powerless to make that artist-type like you. How will you regain your power? By bingeing, purging, or restricting yourself at a later date.

In both cases, you took one specific incident—buying the wrong bikini or dating the wrong person—and turned it into a rule for life. Here are some methods to overcome overgeneralization in the future:

1. *Get rid of the absolutes.* Quit using words like all, every, none, nobody, everybody, never, always, etc. to describe your life. Although it is easier to say that "all people do this" or "nobody likes that," rarely is this the case.

2. *Avoid statements about the future.* For starters, recovery begins today, not tomorrow. More specifically, you have no way of predicting the future.

Filtering:

I love the concept of filtering, although I despise the results. Filtering is so common for those of us with EDs. In particular, we often filter out the good and let in only the bad. For example, the positive self-talk always gets filtered out in favor of the negative self-talk. Typically, the negative is all we hear!

An example of filtering would be if you cooked Thanksgiving dinner for the whole family for the first time in your new apartment. You spent weeks preparing everything down to the detail. Each person got their own plastic turkey place card holder, the spinach was organic, the pies fresh made, and the turkey delectable.

Unfortunately, you forgot the fried onion topping for the green bean casserole and you were forced to go to the corner store for a back-up can at the last minute. But the back-up can was three years old! So one person out of twelve said, "What a meal! If only the green bean casserole had been fresher!"

The result of filtering is that all you hear is the negative. By extrapolation, the entire experience becomes negative. All you hear is the one bad review. Not the raves about the plastic turkeys or the correct spellings on the place cards or the hand woven tablecloth or the perfectly juicy turkey or the delectable mashed potatoes (from scratch). Sound familiar? And, for goodness sakes—don't start purging because of this critique! By all accounts, the evening was superb! Here are some ways to rebut filtering:

1. *Look for balance.* When you hear a negative comment, immediately train yourself to look for the good. Let's say someone praises you for your work performance but comments that you are often late to work. Don't just hear, "You're late to work; you're a big, fat, loser." Hear the good and the bad and try focusing on your strength for once, instead of your weakness.

2. *Look for the opposite of what you typically filter for.* For example, if you tend to focus on loss, make up rebuttals that stress all the good things that have not been lost. If you see rejection all around you, write descriptions of the times when you were accepted and loved.

Polarized Thinking:

This is a fancy way of saying you see everything—*everything*—in black and white, with no shades of gray. Here, people are good or bad, never a little bit of both (as is most often the case). You are either beautiful or ugly, never how you really look. Another way to term this would be to call it "absolute" thinking; you see everything in this or that extreme, not what lies between; your world is full of absolutes.

Let's say you think pizza is bad for you. Never mind that if you get the thin crust it may be a bit less caloric for you than the deep dish; forget that if you get all vegetables on top it's probably also less caloric than if you get the meat lover's super supreme.

By the principle of polarization, pizza is all bad, all the time. So what happens when you finally succumb and have a piece? And then two more in rapid succession? *You* are bad, by association. Not momentarily weak or human, not hungry or experiencing a unique craving, not in a hurry or low on cash … but B-A-D! Can you see now why polarization might not be the healthiest of behaviors? Why, then, would polarization be so bad for us ED victims? You guessed it! Because you only see things in black and white, and you just ate a piece of "bad" pizza … yup … here comes that binge, purge, restriction cycle all over again! Gosh, ED … go away!

Rebuttals to polarized thinking include the following:

1. *Be more precise.* It's easier to over generalize by saying something is all good or all bad. It's harder to be more specific, but when you do those walls of polarization come tumbling down. Why not take a look at all of the angles? It's actually kind of fun to look at things from every point of view!

2. *Be a mathematician.* Score yourself in terms of percentages, such as twenty-five percent or fifty percent or seventy-five percent. (We are rarely one hundred percent of anything.) For instance, in our pizza example, if there are five slices of pizza and you ate three of them, then you are not one hundred percent "bad" but only sixty percent "bad." (While I *strongly* disavow myself from the word "bad," it's still better than considering yourself a total washout because you had three lousy pieces of pizza!) Heck, if you eat the pizza, enjoy it without the guilt. We have to remind ourselves that, in and of itself, pizza is *not bad.* That's the whole point: the self-talk and the emotion of guilt are precisely what send you spiraling back to ED!

Self-Blame:

Pretty self-explanatory, this one: This is when you chastise yourself for everything, not just for your own shortcomings (as you perceive them to be), but things completely out of your control as well, such as how others react to you at a party or at work.

I have a nickname for this one, too: "apologizing for yourself." The movie wasn't good? Forget the fact that the acting stunk, the first director was canned halfway through the project (and the second was no better), and no one else who came along bothered to read the reviews. You apologize for suggesting it anyway.

The service at the restaurant was slow? Your fault. Someone gave you the wrong zip code at work so you hold up the line at the post office and what do you do? Apologize. Well, stop it!

Unfortunately, too many of us have more patience for others than we do for ourselves. This is because we are lacking in self-esteem. When we are confident, and recognize our weaknesses as human, we will be more accepting of ourselves, allowing us to be more relaxed and understanding with ourselves and with others. So, when we are constantly blaming ourselves for everything, we naturally tend to self-destruct in a way that reinforces our ED, by … doing what? You guessed it: bingeing, purging, restricting, etc.

Some rebuttals to self-blame are included here:

1. *Hit the pause button.* Count to ten before you use the words "I'm sorry." It's simple, but it works. By number five, you'll usually have the same reaction: "Hey, wait a minute, it wasn't my fault the movie stunk/restaurant was slow/the zip code was bad/…whatever"

2. *Shift the focus. You* are not the center of the universe nor the reason for all the world's failures. When you stop taking responsibility for all that ails the world, you will find it easier to stop accepting so much blame as well.

3. *Empower yourself:* People who feel powerful don't assume they're to blame as often as those who feel powerless. Give yourself more power by using positive statements such as, "I may have suggested the movie but no one else made any alternative choices. At least I spoke up and made a firm decision!"

Personalization:

Ah, another favorite with the ED crowd! So what is personalization? Think of it this way: you go to Starbucks and order a cup of coffee and the cashier can barely hear you because you're so worried that everyone is listening to you that you keep your voice real low. Listening to you? Been to a coffee shop lately?

Those people couldn't care less what you're ordering, let alone what you're *saying*.

Another form of personalization is to go to the beach and immediately begin comparing everyone else on the sand to you: taller, thinner, shorter, curvier, blonder, better tan, worse skin, or whatever. In laymen's terms, personalization is thinking you are the center of the wheel, instead of the many spokes that hold the wheel together.

My patients particularly enjoy the benefits of personalization, which is where you think you are the center of the universe (otherwise known in less subtle terms as *narcissism*). It's human nature, of course, to think that everything that happens on this planet is somehow related to you, but when you continue to think that everything always has to do with you it becomes quite narcissistic.

I always tell my patients how narcissistic they are. I let them know that other people couldn't care less what they look like because they are too insecure and only worried about what *they* look like!

Why do some of us think that everything is centered around us? Kind of strange to think you have that much power over others, isn't it? Why do we do this? Is everyone else trying to compare themselves to you? Well, if they all suffer from ED, maybe. But who really cares what *you* are wearing or fixates on what you look like?

Why in the world do we constantly compare ourselves to others like this? Is it not true that we all have unique qualities that others do not possess? Then why are we so eager to be like (we think) others are? The grass may seem greener on the other side of the fence. But, trust me, I've been on both sides, and mine is the prettiest … from the inside out!

And guess what else? Not everyone is always judging. We are only projecting this because it is what *we* are worried about! Think about that! At any given moment we could be bigger, smaller, prettier, uglier, smarter, less intelligent, richer, or poorer than the person next to us. Why in the world would we want to drive ourselves crazy every moment of our lives comparing like that? Let's just be who we are, if only for a moment. Feel it. It's so liberating!

Here are some ways to refute personalization:

1. *Remember the snowflakes.* If you are constantly comparing yourself to others, your rebuttal should stress that people are unique and that we all have different strengths and weaknesses.

2. *Concentrate on affirming your own right to be exactly as you are, without apology or judgment.* Enjoy and appreciate your uniqueness and stop trying to live up to other people's standards. (After all, the "others" you're thinking are so beautiful, rich, powerful, and happy are probably not as happy, or beautiful, rich and powerful, as we perceive them to be!) They're probably saying the same thing about you! So, get out there and act the part!

3. *We are all little fish in a big pond.* Lastly, realize that most of what goes on in the world has nothing to do with you (as hard as that is to believe sometimes)!

Mind Reading:

Finally, we get to a very common cognitive distortion, or *bent thought*, which is "mind reading." This habit of mind is very irrational and far from having ESP. In this case of bent thinking you automatically assume that everyone in the world is thinking *just like you.* Everyone must love your favorite band, and how can everyone not love that new restaurant down the block, and this new lipstick is the absolute best, and why didn't your favorite movie win the Oscar because everyone *must* have loved it?

How is mind reading indicative of an ED? Well, it may sound fairly harmless, but mind reading actually feeds into our negative self-talk more than you might imagine. Just think about it: if everyone thinks exactly like *you* do, and *you* think you're a big, fat, lazy, worthless, insignificant slob, then so must everybody else! Everywhere you go, all day long, your mind is reading these negative thoughts about *you.* There is no escape; these thoughts are everywhere! Can you see now how harmful that might be?

Here is what to do to avoid mind-reading:

1. *Be specific and accurate.* Whenever you feel yourself assuming something about someone, ask yourself why and list the evidence for it. More often than not, you'll find you were pretty far off base about both!

2. *Ask and you shall receive.* Realize that you have no way of knowing what they are thinking unless you inquire.

3. *Assume nothing.* By not assuming anything, you are on a fact-finding mission every day. The key word there being "fact." When you deal in facts rather than assumptions (the rational versus the irrational), your

knowledge base grows exponentially, and the way you see the world shrinks to what is real and accurate, not biased and perceived.

Can you perhaps see now why these are called "distortions?" We should try to avoid such thoughts if at all possible. Of course, we all know it's hard to go "cold turkey," particularly when many of these behaviors have had our entire lives to build up.

That is why we treat this as an exercise, rather than an experiment. Practice the healthier behaviors and execute them when you feel the ED mindset kicking in. Use the alternatives I've suggested as a guide, not an absolute. The templates I offer you are just suggestions. Every patient internalizes the information and naturally adapts it to her own comfort level. Some patients use the templates verbatim; others change them liberally. Some accomplish the task of "straightening out" their "bent thought" more quickly, while others take their time, allowing the new way of thinking to penetrate the old before turning the screws.

Remember this: the ED is yours, so the choices are yours. I want you to succeed on your schedule, following your timetable. You know yourself better than anybody. You must take some personal accountability for playing your part in kicking ED to the curb, just as you must be active and vigilant about watching out for those silent "triggers" that help your ED to flare up from time to time.

Negative self-talk, irrational thinking, and cognitive distortions have all been programmed and planted into our psyches. We need to make the unconscious conscious and prepare for war. The choice is yours. Let's win this war against ED together!

Letters to ED, to our bodies, to ourselves:

Dear ED,

Although you have become my daily companion, never leaving my thoughts, actions, and body, I truly hate you. I have let you take control of me and you are destroying my life. Because of you I have lost my goals, ambition, confidence, and self-respect. Because of you I have become estranged from my friends and family. Because of you I have isolated myself from the whole world, other than my abusive boyfriend. Because of you I am not the person I used to be. I had potential and a fire inside of me until you got a hold of me.

The scariest part is that because you have ruled my life for so many years the real me is becoming such a faint memory. I used to be on top of the world, and nobody was going to stop me from doing everything I wanted to do, achieving all my goals. Whoever would have thought that feisty girl would have succumbed to something less than a person. I miss the me before you, and so do all the people that love me. Because of you I am no longer me, the person I used to be. This is not my life; it's not what it was before.

You are a drug, an addiction, and nemesis. You are my worst enemy yet ever faithful by my side. I hate you and I wish you would just die. I've never hated someone before or said such harsh things. But you aren't a person, you don't have to exist. You are the devil. I created you and I will destroy you before you destroy me. Go to Hell, ED!

Yours in wellness,

"Tracey"

CHAPTER 4

The Human Tightrope

(Perception, Reality and the Life Lived Between)

"In the century now dawning, spirituality, visionary conscious-
ness, and the ability to build and mend human relationships will
be more important for the fate and safety of this nation than our
capacity to forcefully subdue an enemy. Creating the world we
want is a much more subtle but more powerful mode of opera-
tion than destroying the one we don't want."

—Marianne Williamson

As we begin to wrap up our discussion of psychological theories, dear reader, we are beginning to move away from the textbook and closer to the reader. (That's *you*, by the way!) This chapter discusses Humanistic Psychology. Key word there being: H-U-M-A-N. (That's *you*, by the way!)

This psychological theory, and this chapter, revolves around two things: perception and reality. Many of us feel these subjects are quite similar. The belief that our perception quite literally defines our reality is at the heart of humanistic psychology.

Humanistic psychology emphasizes individual choice and responsibility. Inherent in the doctrine is a human's ability to choose; free will means we can take in information and do with it what we please; we can choose to act on it; or choose to *not* act on it. We can respond to stimuli, or choose not to respond. Choosing *not* to act is a response in and of itself.

Isn't that how we live our day? We get up in the morning, and it's pouring rain outside. Hmm, what does this mean? First, let's take in some information: for starters, no morning jog, no trip to the nearby racquetball court, no big deal. I wanted a few extra minutes of sleep anyway. So we actually just perceived the rain to be OK *if* we decided we wanted to stay in and sleep, right? Our perception here becomes positive. Are you with me so far? So far, so good, right?

Later, we process some other information (our cognitions at work): bring an umbrella, don't wear that pretty new suede skirt, or we might as well dry our hair curly. Finally, we take some very specific actions based on that perception: we grab our raincoat, make sure our wipers work, and drive extra carefully.

That's how it's *supposed* to work, anyway. But let's peer into the mind of someone who lives with ED. We wake up, see it's raining, and immediately our perception turns our reality into disaster:

> Darn it, I can't jog, that means I'll have to restrict myself to 500 fewer calories at lunch than I was planning on. Oh, woe is me. Why does this always happen to me? Maybe I can go to the gym? No, no, I don't belong there. Everyone will look at me, see how fat I am, how worthless I am. God, why did it have to rain? I bet it's not raining in Hollywood. I bet all those beautiful, skinny stars are outside, right now, running to their heart's content. God, they're so lucky. What did I ever do to deserve this crummy life? Oh, that's right: I do deserve this crummy life …

OK, that's the process and perception part. Then how do we behave for the rest of the day?

I think you know the answer to that one …

Make self-fulfillment a self-fulfilling prophecy

Humanistic psychology relates to most people's idea of what being human means because the theory places value on personal ideals and self-fulfillment. Every day we act in accordance with our own set of personal ideals and self-fulfillment. These are different for every single individual on this planet. We are all unique.

We might want to reach a certain weight, earn a certain amount of money, earn a certain grade, meet a certain man, buy a certain house, or send out a certain message. As humans, we strive to contribute; we are compelled to do more and more until we are satisfied. At the heart of humanistic psychology is the individual; it applies to the human first. It subscribes to the theory that we are always striving to reach our fullest potentials, and there is never an end point to our evolution. After all, this is an ongoing process, always evolving.

Humanistic psychology considers a person in the context of his environment and in conjunction with his personal perceptions and feelings. In essence, none of us live in a vacuum. Yes, we have our personal ideals and goals of self-fulfillment, but we are surrounded by and affected by a society that we cannot exist outside. Society sends us messages about how much we *should* earn, what we *should* accomplish, how much we *should* weigh, people we *should* admire, or with whom we *should* socialize.

All day long we, as humans, are naturally in conflict with other humans. The choices we make are often tainted by the actions of others. What happened to us in the past echoes through our current thoughts, self-talk, and self-fulfillment, for better or worse. Our past, and in particular how we feel about the past—that chemical makeup of previous hurts, happiness, hope, and hopelessness—make up what the psychiatric community refers to as our cognitive schema.

What's better? What's worse? Are we good? Bad? Fat? Thin? Pretty? Ugly? Who's to say? Seriously, I'm asking this question: who's to say? What defines beauty? Heavy? Ugly? Smart? Do scientists define these things? Do friends, family, or teachers decide on the definitions?

The bottom line is that our perception gets colored by a multitude of sources, and our perception, in turn, defines our reality. This basically means that how you view things is only *your* reality and not necessarily anyone else's. Think about that for a minute. Interesting, huh? There are as many realities in this world as there are people. That's why humanistic psychology is so important.

The chief, the ships, and perception, or if it matters to you, it matters!

Whether perception is accurate or not is irrelevant. Think of it this way: years ago an ancient culture lived on an island in the Pacific Ocean. Cut off from society, left to their own devices, they created a thriving and vibrant culture that reflected their shared, collective values of self-perception and self-fulfillment. Their bellies were full of fish and fresh vegetables, the scant clothing they wore protected sensitive areas and served a purpose, their colorful body paint identified them by rank and file, and all was good in the world.

Then the chief, who stood watch on a high cliff at a certain time each day, noticed something strange in the water, there, out on the horizon. What was it? Simple, flowing ripples, but ripples that didn't used to be there. They weren't there when he was a child, standing near his father as the former chief watched the water.

So the chief watched the water every day, and every day he watched more closely, until finally details began to materialize. This chief knew nothing of ships. He knew not of trade winds or spice-islands or trade routes or barter or money. But the shapes he began to see were ships, and so he came to know ships, to describe ships to his people, to point the ships out to them, and day by day, more of them could see these ships. Finally, their civilization knew the meaning of that thing called ship.

Until he could define for himself the meaning of ships, they did not exist for the chief. That was the chief's reality. In the same way, according to humanistic psychology, the realities that have become our cognitive schema affect what we know/perceive to be real.

Humanistic psychology is not a true science because it involves too much common sense and not enough objectivity. So why do I include it here? It gives me the opportunity to talk about what is so ingrained in the typical ED sufferer's life: a warped sense of reality.

Humanistic psychology lets us peer into this world and talk more about perception and how it relates to our day, our weight, our appearance, our overall image, our history, ourselves, and our lives. In many ways, to most humans in general and definitely to sufferers of ED in particular, perception truly is paramount.

If you perceive things in a negative manner, you will begin acting in the same way. Look at it this way: you wake up one morning and look in the mirror. You say to yourself, "I am so ugly and fat. I am such a loser." How do you think the rest of your day will go?

That negative perception ripples through your day, affecting how you dress, how you sit up or slouch down, how you approach people, how you perform in school or at work, how you perceive people's reaction to you, and even how you sleep at night. When the negative perception persists long enough, it *becomes* your reality.

You don't just think you're a big, fat loser; you become a big, fat loser in your reality. It is more delusional than a self-fulfilling prophecy; it is patent fiction. Even if you weigh three hundred pounds you are *not* a big, fat loser. That is not reality. Weight and winning have nothing to do with one another. They are apples and oranges. Unfortunately, perception and reality are not so easy to distinguish.

Now what if, rather, you said to yourself, "I feel *great!* I am a beautiful person inside and out, and this day is going to be better than yesterday!" Big difference in the way your day will unfold, right? Those positive vibes will echo in everything you do: your dress, your driving, your desires, and your diplomacy. Will your smile be brighter? Yes. Will you dress better? Yes. Will you feel better? Yes! And, one thing is certain: you will be happier, and you will not only make a difference in your life, you will also make a difference in the world around you.

We exude confidence and pride from the inside out.

The job interview: an experiment in two parts

Let's put it into a clearer perspective by using this little experiment: Negative Nelly wakes up on Monday morning at the same time as Positive Polly. Both are high school graduates looking for a summer job at Company ABC. They are both young, bright, attractive women.

Negative Nelly wakes up and says, "I don't even know why I'm wasting my time. My hair is limp, my thighs are curdling, and my butt is fat. My chest? Forget it. I have nothing to wear, my car needs an oil change, my leather valise is cracked, and my resume sucks. I should just go back to bed."

Negative Nelly won't go back to bed. (It would almost be better if she did!) Her perception is so warped and dismal that she must reinforce it to define her own reality. She has to perform poorly to reemphasize how bad her life sucks! So she dresses in the same drab power suit she's worn to a dozen other failed interviews that summer, does her hair in the same tired, dowdy manner, and drives her chugging car to the parking lot of Company ABC where she greets the receptionist with a perfunctory air and answers the interviewer's questions by rote, merely going through the motions so that she can zip back home and wait for the phone call that never comes.

And what of Positive Polly? She wakes up about an hour before Negative Nelly. Why? So she can do her morning affirmations, get in her thirty-minute meditation session, have a great breakfast, and still shower and primp before getting in her freshly pressed power suit before driving her equally sluggish, but twice as colorful, car to Company ABC.

There she greets the receptionist with an enthusiastic smile and a kind word about her wedding ring or lip gloss. She makes the same kind of positive, enthusiastic impact on her interviewer, who notes in the margins of her resume, "Enthusiastic! A go-getter! Call back?" before she even answers question one.

How do you think the interview goes for Positive Polly? How do you think she answers questions asked by the interviewer? How do you think she presents herself? Holds herself? Positively, right?

And who do you think got the job? Does it really matter? If Negative Nelly got the job, how long do you think she'd last before her negative attitude infected the entire division and got her canned? If Positive Polly didn't get the job, how long do you think it would be before she got a different one?

What is reality?

What is perception?

Negative Nelly's perception is that she's a failure, so she creates that reality for herself. Even when good things happen, they are either a mistake or she doesn't deserve them. What will she do as a result? She will sabotage herself, sucking the positivity, life, and potential out of any good news until, at last, aha, there's that bad news she was waiting for!

And Positive Polly? What's her reality? From an interviewer's standpoint, Polly might not be totally qualified for the job, didn't go to a school as good as some of the other candidates, and might lack the maturity to fill the job correctly. Based on those realities, he might not have hired her. (Although he probably made himself a note to contact her if the person he does hire doesn't work out!)

However, the interviewer may have held the common belief that "attitude is everything!" He might have hired Polly based on her attitude alone, recognizing that her can-do spirit and positive nature would easily make her more than trainable for the position he had in mind—or just about any other position his company might offer Polly some day. (Including his own!)

For Polly, no matter the outcome of the interview, the reality is that she knows she can gain all those skills she is currently lacking, on the job or off. If the interviewer doesn't hire her, she doesn't kick herself for losing out on a job or use her emotional baggage to explain why. If she is hired, she recognizes the valuable opportunity in her path and treats it with all the respect and enthusiasm it deserves. She takes each interview on a case-by-case basis because her parents, peers, weight, and self-talk don't matter to the interviewer. Her positivity does.

In the end, her positivity remains intact.

My perception; my reality

Remember how my family uprooted me and we moved to Syracuse just before my sixteenth birthday? How do you think that affected my own perception of the world? Of myself? Of my family? Of Syracuse? Of my neighborhood?

I'll put it this way: the girls at school hated me. Why? Who knows? It might have been because I hated me. Life could have been very different if my perception of myself had been better. I might have smiled more, had more confidence to introduce myself to more people, and possibly made more friends, in turn affecting how I thought of myself for the next couple of decades.

Fact is, we'll never know. I wasn't confident, wasn't happy, and my perception was grim, so my reality evolved to match. I became isolated, shy, and depressed. I did befriend one other girl, who was kind of an outcast herself. Gradually, we became best of friends, uniting together in our teenage angst and fighting the world, "us against them."

We eventually became bulimic together.

Yep, my friend and I would just eat everything in sight (and my mother had a kitchen full of food at all times; she fed the entire neighborhood, and prided herself on that) and then we'd just puke. Sounds like lots of fun, huh?

I lived next to the high school in a very exclusive neighborhood, so people assumed we were rich. You'd think that would make me more popular, right? Wrong. It only alienated me all the more, which only fed into my negative perception, which in turn fed my negative reality that life had always sucked, sucked now, and would always suck. What to do about it?

I binged, I purged, sometimes with my similarly outcast friend, sometimes alone. It gave me power; it gave me control. For a few minutes a few times each day life didn't suck. ED made sure of that.

But then the guilt, and reality, would wash back over me. I wasn't powerful, wasn't smarter than everybody else, and would never be liked, let alone loved. So I began seeking more power. I started playing tennis; I played partly to control my weight, partly to just plain control ... something. Naturally, I pursued tennis with a vengeance and became number one on the girls' tennis team. I dated guys, hated them, and hated myself for hating them for hating me. It was made all the more dismal by the perception from which I viewed the entire world: my sick, twisted, lonely world.

And if I perceived myself poorly, you can only imagine the way others, particularly those girls I envied and yet hated, perceived me. Well, what did I know about perception? All I knew is how Doctor #2 had discouraged me back in Milwaukee and that I had just been uprooted from my boyfriend and moved across the country. I knew that my mother hated me, I had no friends, I had started a new school, I was all alone in my own twisted world, I got cut from the cheerleading squad (to my mother's dismay), and … now I was in Syracuse with Mom and Nana. Stranded, no one to turn to, all alone.

Except, of course, for ED.

Perception and reality viewed through the lens of time

Two years later at a graduation party, the popular girls told me I was "pretty cool after all," and they apologized to me for being mean for two years. Who to believe? Turns out the popular girls' perception of me was that I was *stuck up*! Me! They thought I was a snob! After all, I guess I had dated their boy friends, lived in a beautiful home where one of the favorite families had lived previous to my family's arrival, and they thought I was pretty! Ha! Did you hear that? I nearly fainted when I heard that.

If life was like a tennis court and I was on one side and they (the popular girls) were on another, then perception was the tennis ball getting whacked back and forth every day. They perceived me as pretty, stuck up, athletic, and smart and so they *treated me badly*. I perceived myself as ugly, fat, unattractive, unadorned, worthless, and unloved, and so I *treated myself badly*!

All along my perception was my reality and it directed my behavior, causing me to self-destruct in ways that damaged my mind, body, and soul. Meanwhile they treated me according to their perception, alienating me, ignoring me, resenting me, and envying me! Talk about a mix up; talk about a sad turn of events and a future of lower self-esteem and a nearly endless journey with my ED!

But guess what happened? Because they now thought I was cool, you would think I'd stop self-destructing, right? I would realize the error of my ways and turn my life around? I would start seeing myself the way others saw me? I would realize I was beautiful, young, and strong and stop bingeing and purging?

Wrong: I used ED even more! (I'll bet some of you readers know *exactly* what I am talking about.) The setup was just too much to resist. For one, I'd been positively reinforced by their reaction (think back to chapter one) for starving and purging: they'd said I was pretty.

Cause: bingeing and purging.

Effect: people say I'm pretty *and* cool.

With all the "what if's" in my life ("what if" my family moves again, "what if" my mother never loves me, "what if" I fail again) this cause and effect was the only reality I knew.

I figured I had to keep up the good work!

So, c'mon ED, let's get back on board!

Negative Nelly or positive Polly

Sound familiar yet? Enough about me, how about you? How does *your* perception affect your behavior? Are you Negative Nelly or Positive Polly? Better yet, how do the perceptions of others affect your behavior? Are there people you are trying to please, never bothering to ask them if what *you* think *they* think of *you* is actually accurate?

Are you constantly trying to please Mom or Dad, your boyfriend or girlfriend, your coaches or siblings? Maybe it's time to realize that the only person you can genuinely please is yourself. We are only responsible for ourselves and our own happiness. Heal thyself; be a role model through your actions. The happiness of others is their choice; not your responsibility. When your perceptions are congruent with your good health, game over: you win!

My point here is this: what will happen if we stop worrying so much about what others think of us and start deciding who we are, what we want, what we feel, and how *we* feel comfortable? Why live up to others' standards when they are all different? Whose rules and perceptions are we supposed to live by? Don't they change every other minute? Person to person? Culture to culture? Decade to decade?

After all, in the fifties and sixties there was no bigger sex symbol than Marilyn Monroe. Women envied her, men lusted after her, and she brought a nation to its feet, tongues wagging every time she walked into a room ... wearing a size-twelve dress. Not size six or four, and definitely not size zero, which is today's ideal.

Have we all gone crazy? How could the ideal from thirty to forty years ago be so wildly different, to the tune of some twelve sizes? To find an answer, just think how the media slowly but steadily impacts our daily life. If we're shown an image of a woman in a size-twelve dress and told daily that she's sexy, aren't we likely to believe that this woman really is sexy?

How can we not? But that's not what we're told anymore. Is it arbitrary? It must be; I can tell it certainly isn't for health reasons. An average size-twelve woman is more likely to be healthy than a woman wearing a size zero. So who decides? Is it Hollywood? *Vogue* magazine? Calvin Klein? *The Today Show? People? Teen?* The answer is yes, to all of the above.

This is why it's so important to start changing our own perspective of one person and one person only: our own self. *We* must decide what's right for us. Let's face it: some of us will never, ever, not in a million years be able to conform to society's current, fleeting idea of what is beautiful and desirous any more than a natural size zero woman could possibly conform to Marilyn Monroe's size-twelve ideal. And, that's OK.

Did you hear me? That's *OK.* We have to be perfectly OK with that! It took me over twenty years of my life to be OK with my natural body type. Please don't waste another day of your lives the way I did! It's just not worth it! The preoccupation is *not worth* the energy or the loss of living it's costing you!

The tides of change are more fortunate for some women over others, but only if you allow the tidal wave of public opinion to wash over you all day, every day.

Our height, our bone structure, our race, our skin tone, or the amount of time in a day we have to devote to exercising, shopping, and moisturizing, it all limits the size we can eventually become—or in fact are *supposed* to be. And what fad are we chasing, anyway? Remember a few years ago when the curvaceous and shapely J-Lo was all the rage? Now it's stick figures like certain hotel heiresses and their adoring entourages. Which fad are we to follow?

And, more importantly, at what cost?

The battle for our self-image

Much like our self-talk defines us, our self-image designs us. Remember: we create our own reality. You, and you alone, wake up in the morning and design your day. Will it be good or bad? Will you smile, frown, binge, purge, or restrict? Will you wear mourning colors or "morning" colors? Yes, real problems affect us; disasters loom. But those of us who befriend ED view each day as a disaster, whether it's our birthday, New Year's Eve, Christmas, or the day we win the lottery!

Of course, I'm hardly one to throw the first stone; from the day I was born, Nana perceived me as a blonde-haired, blue-eyed ball of perfection. My mother handed me to her and that was that. From that day on, I was Nana's little darling. Mom ignored me and was jealous of me, and Nana controlled me. Her perception-expectation of me was that I would be married to a doctor or lawyer and be "taken care of." That was her perception; that was her reality. It soon became my perception and my reality.

I was different from my mother in every physical way. I had blonde, wavy hair, pale skin and blue eyes. Mom had black curly hair, dark skin, and brown eyes. Nana loved the Aryan look, as she perceived that was the *ideal* look. So, essentially, if you think about it, I grew up with ED from day one.

Why? The cause and effect relationship I had with Nana began from early childhood, only to be reinforced later by the girls at school, who praised me (effect) for the way I kept my appearance through restricting, bingeing, and purging (cause). I got the same effect from Nana: her only praise came from when I looked the way she perceived I *should* look; blond-haired, blue-eyed, rail thin, as was the style growing up. Any slight deviation—baby fat, pudgy cheeks, growth spurt, too athletic, too masculine—produced a negative reaction.

I learned that I could control Nana's reaction by controlling myself; it was the only control I had, the only power I had, and the only happiness I had. Nana's perception was that I had to keep my appearance, so ED kept me under control. Nana made sure that I had to cultivate ED in order to keep my appearances. It was the only way a healthy, normal, growing American girl could keep getting the positive reinforcement from the only adult figure who loved her: starve and make Nana happy; make Nana happy and you, too, can be happy.

Gain a pound, grow an inch, go up a size, and that last adult figure who really cared would be unhappy. We couldn't have that now, could we? And just why did this hurt me so much? Well, let the story begin: Mom was always jealous of me. So she always said things that hurt ... things that hurt to this day.

One day I came in after school and I overheard her in her bedroom, crying on the phone with her best friend, saying, "I can't stand Susie. I wish I never had a daughter ..." Her perception of me was that I was a horrible daughter. I was too flawed, and I shouldn't be in existence. Well, that was my perception of what she was saying. Tell me what you would have perceived! Guess what I did? Well, you know ... c'mon! ED was my only friend ... take a guess!

One year I had a wonderful boyfriend from New Jersey. He flew to Syracuse for Christmas when I came home from college. He gave me a Paddington Teddy Bear and on the neck of the bear was a diamond and ruby necklace. When my mother saw it she said to him, "Why did you do that? Susie doesn't deserve that!" Her perception of me was, once again, that I was unworthy ... I was worthless ... I was trash.

The only person that I was worthy of was ED.

My mother, being unhappy herself, took her misery out on me. It really didn't help matters much that she felt jealous that her own mother had a stronger bond with me than she had with her. It was a bit uncomfortable, to say the least.

You see, it made my mother's perception of me so much more negative, which then caused me to act in more destructive ways. It just made matters worse all the way around. Trying to keep the peace and please them both was nearly impossible. Protecting the feelings of both of them? Ha, it was practically impossible.

So, naturally, ED helped me maintain some control over the situation. If any of you reading this book are mothers yourselves, please don't take out your own past or your own pain on your daughters, especially if they have or are prone to EDs. This is so counterproductive and can prove to be fatal. My suggestion to the mothers out there is this: please resolve your own issues with a trained professional. This will not only benefit you, but your child as well.

Perception is an imperfect science

OK, back to this perception stuff. Mom used to always to tell me, "I can see you marrying a doctor and going to all of the physician's black tie parties." Ha! If they only knew the kinds of guys I was dating! ED for one! And all of the other guys I would pick up that were uneducated, and lower than low, just to have some company for only a little while … to just feel like "somebody" for once.

Well, of course, my lower than low self-esteem was killing every ounce of my soul, my psyche, and my body. Why is this so important for you to know? Well, because if Mom and Nana perceived me to be with great, wonderful men then, of course, I needed to hide the fact that I was dating the losers. So, what do you think I needed to do to regain control of myself? Yep, you guessed it! Befriend ED again and dump the other guys! I mean, what nice guy would want me anyway?

Actually, I think everyone sent me to college to get an M.R.S. degree (Mrs.… get it?)

I did actually date an MD later on in my life. Yes, I did! Just after one of my boyfriends punched me in the face and broke my nose! I ended up having the cartilage in my nose moved over and the only unattached doctor in the hospital ended up being my anesthesiologist! I was working in the rehab part of the hospital at the time as a director of therapeutic recreation (although I was only twenty-three at the time). Once I returned to work, there was a note on my desk asking me to go out with him … the anesthesiologist!

Well, I couldn't have that. A good man, a doctor no less, going out with unworthy me? Not on your life. After summarily rejecting him several times, however, I finally gave in. I started dating him, and guess what? He cheated on me over and over (and did many other despicable things that I will not discuss in this book). Now, *that's* what I call a great guy! So, guess who I ended up going back to? ED! ED was always there for me! My best friend!

After I broke up with this doctor, Nana was upset because she had been thrilled that her granddaughter was dating a doctor. Finally, an upstanding doctor! And what had I done? Gone and ruined it. According to her, it just had to be my fault. Perception in the community is everything, of course. Forget about the cheating, the betrayal, the degradation, etc. He was a D-O-C-T-O-R. Wasn't that worth putting up with all the rest?

Unfortunately, the challenges of perception continue long after our childhood. Despite what I may have done to grow, progress, and change, I am still held captive by certain archaic beliefs shared by many family members back home.

Case in point: I was recently speaking to Nana (now called Sally) when she said, "Did you see that girl (referring to the Olsen twin with anorexia)? I was wondering how she kept such a beautiful figure!"

Argh! I was about to strangle her through the phone. Does that woman have no clue about EDs? Even after all this time? Even with a granddaughter who is a therapist who specializes in them? Sally actually believes that a girl with anorexia is beautiful and she wanted to know why I couldn't have a figure like that! And, you know what? That's her problem. Not mine anymore. It's just way too challenging to even try to teach her at this point. The woman is 89 years old and so stuck in her superficial ways that it would do no good to try to educate her at this point. Fortunately, although she can still manage to ruffle my feathers and shoot my blood pressure sky high, she can never penetrate *my* psyche again! And, thanks to my new perception—my new, healthy reality—this conversation did *not* send me back into ED's arms and will certainly never do so!

On another recent occasion, when I flew to Florida to visit Sally on the way to meeting my editor for this book, within the first thirty-six hours in her presence, she made no less than forty-seven comments (yes, I counted!) referring to looks, beauty, thinness, and appearance. She even had the nerve to say that she couldn't stand Katie Couric (that's the same weekend that the news came out that Katie was offered a job as the first woman solo anchor).

When I asked her why she didn't like good old Katie (and who doesn't like good old Katie?), Sally replied, "Look at her hair and her clothes. She looks terrible."

I had to butt in on this one. I said, "Does that take away from her ability to perform her job as a newscaster?" My goodness! I mean really! So, what did I decide to do? Not ED this time! For once, I chose to interpret this in a healthier manner. I didn't interpret it as I would have back in the olden days when I would have automatically assumed that Sally was indirectly telling me how fat and ugly I was. Nope … I spoke up and spoke my mind and didn't personalize it a bit!

When "looking healthy" becomes a put down

I use these stories to reiterate my driving point: When a person tells someone with anorexia that they look good or healthy, they automatically perceive/internalize that to mean *they are fat*. What's the logical reaction? ED kicks in. Now there is more restricting, over-exercising, or purging.

I guess my point here is that poor Sally may not be able to help herself specifically because she just doesn't realize how harmful and damaging it might be to me or to others. It's so very difficult for anyone, and very frustrating to say the least, for family members and loved ones to know what to say or how to say anything to someone suffering with anorexia, or anyone with any ED for that matter … simply because the person with ED will twist everything. Every word is a landmine; every conversation a minefield.

The smallest of compliments, let alone put downs, has ramifications in the mind of someone with ED that someone without ED could never, ever comprehend. Even when it's about someone else—a super-thin celebrity being referred to as "cute" or a superstar who's gained weight as being "washed up"—can set off a chain reaction that lasts for days, weeks, months, or a lifetime in the mind of a person who befriends ED.

Where does it all derive from? Perception. The person with ED perceives every comment to be directed at her. Her unique world view is that she is fat and everyone knows it, so every comment, be it about celebrities, family members, friends or the lamppost, is directly perceived as an insult, goad, or hidden message reaffirming what she knows to be her own personal reality: she is fat, worthless, and she must enlist her battalion of ED behaviors to compensate.

Part and parcel of the content in this chapter is this basic fact: we all process information differently and, therefore, must work individually with our own psychologists to learn the most effective way to support the patient. There is simply no template of rules to provide to a family member to help their loved one, as each stage of recovery brings with it a different set of rules.

I could go on and on and on, but I'll spare you. My point is this: if I continued to worry about everyone else's perception of me, and I followed their ideals for me, here's what I would probably be doing right now... I'd be divorced (which I am), but without an education and on welfare with about six kids. Or, I'd be six feet under.

Actually, the latter is probably the most likely scenario. ED would have eaten me alive (no pun intended), and I would have either died by the hands of ED, or killed myself, or been beaten to death by my ex-husband (that's a whole other book). Either way, I wouldn't be sitting here writing this book, talking with any of you, or living out the only passion I have ever dreamed of since I was a young girl—to help guide and empower the lives of others in a world where no one else ever seemed to understand *me*.

What the Bleep Do We Know?

In the groundbreaking movie *What the Bleep Do We Know*, several top scientists, gurus, mentors, and mystics reveal the surprising relationship between what we are and what we do, what we think and what we "know." It is an amazing movie-slash-documentary that I "prescribe" to all my patients. Why? I've yet to find a better vehicle for describing the relationship that this whole chapter has been about: perception versus reality. More specifically, if watched carefully and listened to intently, one can glean from this marvelous, majestic, yet simple film all they need to know about choosing a life that's wonderful, freeing, lively, illuminating, and fulfilling.

The most often referenced interview in the film is Dr. Joe Dispenza's comments on creating his day. I include it for you here:

> I wake up in the morning and I consciously create my day the way I want it to happen. Now sometimes, because my mind is examining all the things that I need to get done, it takes me a little bit to settle down and get to the point of where I'm actually intentionally creating my day. But here's the thing: when I create my day and out of nowhere little things happen that are so unexplainable, I know that they are the process or the result of my creation. And the more I do that, the more I build a neural net in my brain that I accept that that's possible. (This) gives me the power and the incentive to do it the next day.
>
> So if we're consciously designing our destiny, and if we're consciously from a spiritual standpoint throwing in with the idea that our thoughts can

affect our reality or affect our life—because reality equals life—then I have this little pact that I have when I create my day. I say, "I'm taking this time to create my day and I'm infecting the quantum field. Now if (it) is in fact the observer's watching me the whole time that I'm doing this and there is a spiritual aspect to myself, then show me a sign today that you paid attention to any one of these things that I created, and bring them in a way that I won't expect, so I'm as surprised at my ability to be able to experience these things. And make it so that I have no doubt that it's come from you," and so I live my life, in a sense, all day long thinking about being a genius or thinking about being the glory and the power of God or thinking about being unconditional love.

I'll use living as a genius, for example. And as I do that during parts of the day, I'll have thoughts that are so amazing, that cause a chill in my physical body, that have come from nowhere. But then I remember that that thought has an associated energy that's produced an effect in my physical body. Now that's a subjective experience, but the truth is that I don't think that unless I was creating my day to have unlimited thought, that that thought would come. (Dr. Joe Dispenza in What the BLEEP Do We Know!? TM)

Go forth … and create your own day

As we close out our discussion of humanistic psychology, I want to charge you with creating tomorrow. Not today, for it is likely half over. Not yesterday, because it is forever gone. But tomorrow lies open and ripe for you, an unwritten page, a blank canvas, a do-over to making better choices than you have in the past.

I don't expect you to cure your ED overnight, climb a mountain, jump out of a plane (oh, but what fun it is!), or even break out of your old routine so quickly. But I *would* like you to wake up and, before doing anything else, consciously create your day.

Think before you act; pause before you slip into old routines and follow the well-worn rut of archaic, destructive behaviors. Think about what you want and how to get it. But do more than think. What will it take to create your day the way you want it to be? Will it take a phone call to your mother? An empowering journey for yourself? A kind word from your boss, love, teacher, coach, mentor, or friend?

What can *you* do—actively, physically—to create your day? I know you're shaking your head right now, thinking this is all some New Age, mumbo jumbo, warm fuzzy come-on to pass the buck from me doing all the work to you doing at least some of it. But what can it hurt? Reading about it simply isn't enough. Application is how it works. It takes baby steps, remember? I already worked through the process. It's your turn now. The journey is yours for the walking.

What can it hurt to be more conscious? To be more aware? To be more curious and inquisitive and experimental with our own lives? How can it hurt to explore what's deep within us? To try and change? Can it hurt more than what you are going through right now? Can it hurt more than repeating the same pattern, day after day? The same pattern that caused you to pick up this book and seek out the information within? It was your free will to pick up this book.

Please, I beg of you: wake tomorrow and create your day. Be conscious of what you perceive and how it affects your reality. Try realistically but persistently to break old habits and shift your perception. All it takes is one small moment, a quick pause to think before you act, and you can consciously reprogram a brain used to cutting you down. You've got free will.

Imagine that: you, a brain re-programmer!

It's possible, it's attainable, and the best part is … it's *your choice!*

Letters to ED, to our bodies, to ourselves:

Dear Body,

How ironic, addressing you as "dear." I don't really treat you like a dear, do I? In fact, if I saw someone treating their child the way I treat you (You are hideous. You disgust me and everyone else. You're so plain and ugly. If you eat that, you can't have anything the rest of the day), I would call child services!

When I think about it, I feel sorry for you, body. No matter how much I curse you, deprive you, and loathe you, my heart still beats, my legs still hold me up, and my lungs still allow me to breath. I could never be that loyal, especially to someone who treated me like absolute shit!

But there are things I hate about you, too. Why can't you be prettier? Taller? Shorter? You're so average (aka plain)! Why can't you let me eat like a normal person and not gain weight? Why do you defy the laws of nutrition and make me gain weight by eating what would be normal for other people? Why do you have to be curvy in some places (thighs and butt) and flat in others (chest)? Why do you have bad skin and big bones and cellulite and weird stray hairs? I'm not asking you to be perfect. Why can't you just be better than average?

I guess I should look at the positive, Body. While you're certainly not turning heads when we walk into a room, you're not turning stomachs either. Plus, no offense, but you're just a shell. I really should be focusing on what's inside. I try very hard to be a good person, and I snagged a good husband and a few good friends, so I can't be all that bad on the inside. You're not getting any younger, and looks don't matter when you're old. What does matter is health, and if I keep abusing you like I have been, you're finally going to rebel and crap out on me.

The truth is, I'm petrified. You made me feel like I was invincible. People would tell me I could die, but my medical tests always came back fine. I secretly wanted them to come back not fine. I felt better when I was sick, because it meant I was a "good" anorexic. Now I'd give anything to feel normal.

Instead, I am in constant fear that you will get back at me for everything I have done to you. Dying is no longer an "if" but a "when." My mind is flooded with questions: What is to keep my heart from just stopping? What if I forget how to breathe? And even worse, the fears have gone into my food habits: What if I am allergic to this food (even though I have had it a million times)? What if I choke? What if, what if, what if?

So, after years of abuse and neglect, I am asking for forgiveness. I hope it's not too late. I will do my best to treat you the way you deserve to be treated, and I hope that you will continue to support me. Like it or not, we're stuck with each other for the rest of our lives. I already know I'm miserable with ED, but I don't know if I would be miserable without him because I haven't tried. With your help, dear body, I would like to give it a go! All in favor say "EYE!" (Blue ones, and they're kind of pretty if I do say so myself ...)

Sincerely,

"Karen"

CHAPTER 5

Forget What You Eat—You Are What You Feel!

Feelings.

Nothing more than feelings.

Trying to forget my feelings of—weight! (I mean, "Wait!") Hold up! Feelings *are* the most important part of human nature! What do you mean "nothing more than feelings?" Feelings are *everything*! Particularly when it comes to EDs. It's *not* about the weight! It's *all* about the feelings!

I know what I did last summer, or what can animated raccoons teach us about our emotions?

And rarely are feelings more important than when it comes to Americans and our food! Case in point: I went to the movies the other day—actually—and decided to skip the pyrotechnics of some of the other summer blockbusters and dive into a lighthearted family fare instead.

What was my choice? *Over the Hedge*, a comical little ditty about a group of foraging critters looking to gorge themselves on our human leftovers and, in the process, learn the true meaning of what it means to be fat ... ehr ... I mean, what it means to be a *family*.

Now, what does an animated children's movie have to do with ED? It has plenty to do with it, just as how our weight has to do with how we *feel*. (Stick with me; I'm actually getting somewhere with this.) Now, as I watched these adorable raccoons, turtles, possums, and squirrels scavenge off the refuse in our trash cans, I found it harder and harder to enjoy myself. After all, here was an entire movie about one thing: food. (And we all know how I feel about food!)

More specifically, how much we as humans *enjoy* food. We crave food, worship food, waste food, horde food, enjoy … well, you get the picture. As one little critter in the movie says: "*We* eat to live; *they* live to eat!" Not a new quote, to be sure, but well into the writing of this book it really hit home: we eat for so many other reasons than mere hunger.

During sadness, gladness, good times, bad times, fun times, and not-so-fun times, we eat. At work, at home, in restaurants, on the way to restaurants, before the movie, during the movie, and after the movie, we eat.

It's the holidays? Let's eat!

Going out on a blind date? Let's eat!

Proposing? Let's eat!

Breaking up? Let's eat!

Getting together with the girls after work? Let's eat!

Bored? Let's eat!

My office drawers are crammed with snack foods "just in case" I get hungry. The break room down the hall and the vending machine on the ground floor are likewise overflowing with plenty of processed goodies just in case we office dwellers go starving in between our 4 to 6 daily meals.

My point here is not to bad mouth summer movies, concession stands, nacho chips, or candy bars. My point here is to say that you and I both know that we eat for a variety of reasons, and little of these have to do with actual hunger, particularly those of us with EDs.

Are you seeing where I'm going with this? If it were merely a matter of "I'm hungry; I'll eat," then we wouldn't be here together because EDs wouldn't exist. If it were a simple matter of "calories in, calories out," the transgabillion-dollar diet industry wouldn't exist. If we all lived on three square meals a day with our *healthy* snacks in between, which we certainly could, vending machines with processed goodies wouldn't exist.

As humans, we are emotional creatures. We think, therefore we act. We feel, so we behave. When our feelings are intense enough, our behavior is to eat. Look at the progression of that simple equation: we feel first, behave second. I'm upset; I eat. I'm feeling insignificant; I don't eat. I'm celebrating; I eat. I'm feeling powerless; I don't eat. Are you seeing a pattern here?

I hope so. I don't mean to sound like a broken record, but I "feel" the need to reinforce what I've said time and time again: It's absolutely, positively, guaranteed, hands down *not about the weight!*

Emotion versus motion

Physically speaking, weight regulation is a very simple process. Food goes in, energy gets expended, the brain sends out a signal to refuel the engines, more food goes in, more energy gets expended, we sleep to rest, wake to eat and add more fuel, and begin the cycle over again.

Emotionally speaking, of course, it's a whole other ball game. So many factors cause us to eat, not eat, binge, purge, and everything in between. What's the first thing you feel before deciding to skip breakfast? Is it powerlessness? Insignificance? Shame? Embarrassment? Alienation?

How about right after you purge? What's your first reaction in that chain of events? Is it guilt? Embarrassment? Worthlessness? Secrecy? More shame? Power? Control? Now let's stop for a minute; look, listen, and rewind. In none of those reactions did you hear physical descriptors: hunger, pain, ache, or satiation. All the reactions, before, during, and after, were emotional ones.

Still think it's all about the weight?

So many books, patients, therapists, articles, journals, parents, family members, and friends make it all about the weight, as if one problem equals one solution. Even if they don't make it about the weight, they think that if they can simply change one behavior they can lick your ED. Well, it's not one magic number (weight) or one magic behavior (action) that will save you.

Instead, it's a combination of many various factors in your life: weight, nutrition, family, balance, knowledge, therapy, emotional health, and psychological wellness. Remember what I said: wellness is a journey, not a destination. We're always so eager to speed things up, get them now, fix them fast, that we forget that the healing comes while we're doing everything else.

The good news is that your journey has already begun. You are already here, present and accounted for, taking that first step after first step. Along the way you have so much to learn, and I want you to look forward to the process, not get discouraged that I didn't present you with a magic number on page one and a magic cure on page two and you're done and well by page three.

That's because recovery from an eating disorder goes much deeper than a mere quick fix. First, we need to pinpoint the genesis of your disease. Where did it start? How far back can we trace its origins? Typically, the strong emotions and heartbreaking framework upon which an ED is built go way, way, *way* back.

This framework often begins in childhood when we start feeling or start thinking, "Wow, there must be something wrong with me. Look how different I am. Look how much more Mom likes the other kids than me. Look how happy everybody else is. What's wrong with me?" These emotions of alienation are the foundation upon which our EDs are built.

Unfortunately, it's not that easy to discuss feelings without talking about behavior, hence all the dogs and bells and clowns and studies we've talked about on the previous pages. Ready for some more?

Well, before we begin I really want to congratulate you on sticking with me so far. It makes me glad that you haven't run away, and I promise you that all of this will help you ... sooner than you think. It just takes a little more time to give you the tools you need to enjoy lifelong recovery versus immediate, unsustainable relief.

If it was so easy, you would have already done it yourself, right?

The nitty-gritty about feelings and emotions

As human beings, we have been blessed and cursed with human emotion! Rarely are two sides of the same coin such opposite ends of the spectrum, but think about it: we have these *really* awesome feelings on one end of the continuum, and the *really* yucky, disturbing emotions on the other end. Haven't you experienced this for yourself?

Sure, come on, I know you have. One minute you're up, the world couldn't be better, the day is your oyster, and nothing's going to stop you from achieving all your dreams and desires. Then, a little later, you forget your feelings of goodwill and are instantly glum. Nothing is right, the world sucks, and who are you to dream in the first place, let alone give into the folly that your puny, insignificant dreams could ever really come true?

It's more than just being emotional.

It's being emotion full ...

Students and patients have long asked me, "Isn't it better to just ignore our feelings; that way we will not let them bother us?" No, no, no. Never, *ever* bury your emotions. (That's what gets us into trouble in the first place!) We've been doing this far too long and look where it's gotten us.

We ended up with ED or other self-destructive behaviors: addictions such as drugs, alcohol, gambling, shopping, sex, Internet, pornography, or other nasty and undesirable behaviors resulting in loss of jobs, broken relationships, anger, violence, flunking out of school, mental illness, and physical illness. Lay them side by side next to each other and you'll see that that whole harrowing list from above is nothing more than a series of escapes and chaos.

And what are we escaping from?

You guessed it: our feelings.

We're feeling down so we drink to forget our feelings; we're feeling good so we drink to celebrate. We use food (bingeing, purging, or restricting) to mask the same uncomfortable emotions. We use food when we feel good, we use food when we feel bad, we use food when we want to feel nothing at all, and we use food when we just want to feel *something*.

Other addictions are just as common. We gamble to feel high. The Internet is a place where for hours on end we can zap aliens, chat with strangers, or gaze at naked pictures and never once feel anything.

Drugs, alcohol, and the rest, they only mask what you're feeling inside; they are temporary fixes to a longstanding problem that is not going to go away until you consciously, actively, and with resolve plan to do something about it. No more suppressing, running away, numbing, or stuffing our feelings! Let's face them head on and learn to *live* once and for all!

If we constantly avoid, run away from, numb, or stuff our emotions, we will mimic robots: simply existing, if that. You see, as humans, we have a gift. That gift is that we *can* feel. We simply have to learn *how* to express and manage emotions in a more effective manner to avoid problems later on.

Suppressing your emotions will only serve to numb your life in every aspect. Experiencing those emotions will allow you to experience not only the pain, but the pleasure that life has to offer as well! To give up the bad is to prevent the good. Talk about throwing out the baby with the bathwater! Don't ever think I don't want you to feel; I just want you to feel better. First off, that means knowing more about why we feel what we feel.

To experience true life is to experience the full range of human emotions: the highs *and* the lows! I sure know that the lows are no fun; I've got plenty of experience in that area. But I will tell you, if you cannot feel the lows, how in the world will you appreciate the highs? To avoid the lows is to cheat yourself of the highs or the good times, too! You *can* have your cake and eat it too!

There's an old Garth Brooks song that puts it perfectly, "Yes, my life is better left to chance. I could have missed the pain but I'd of had to miss the dance ..." I don't want you to miss out on one moment of this life—this dance—but it takes knowing some of the bad to appreciate the good. And the more you know the more control you gain.

Coping is key: feelings can't be avoided, but they can be managed

We may not have direct control over our feelings, but we *do* have control over how we cope with them and how to prevent certain ones—particularly those baddies that make us think ED is really our friend after all—from surfacing too frequently.

In chapters two and three we discussed how to change our thought processes and how to choose our perceptions. These two processes—changing and choosing—are point-blank what effects an eventual change in our emotions. As a review, feelings do not come out of the blue. They are influenced by our thoughts, perceptions, interpretations, memories, and images. Learning to manage our emotions is the foundation for healthy living. It is pertinent to a stable and healthy lifestyle.

You will always have emotions. Let's just get that little nugget out of the way right now. Knowing you will always have emotions, what are we then to do about them? We can't just simply delete the bad ones in favor of the good ones, but we can learn how to handle those emotions that trigger our ED. That is what we will try to do in this chapter; that is your goal for this section of reading material.

E for emotions; B for breakup

During your recovery and breakup from ED, you may notice some unaccustomed emotions that will begin to surface. That's a great word, for they *will* come from under the surface and make their way to the tip of the iceberg, which is just where we want them. It may not be pleasant, but it's vital to your healing.

It is entirely normal to experience feelings more intensely when you begin to face situations that you have been numbing, restricting, constricting, purging, or stuffing for a long time (thanks to your buddy ED). This can often result in what appears to be a *temporary* setback, where acting out behavior results. I stress the word "temporary."

Still, I see the pattern time and time again. Early in their loved one's recovery, many parents or family members come to me and claim that their loved one is getting worse. Who do they blame? Me, of course. But that's OK; I understand all too well the need to displace blame onto the closest and most likely target. After all, I'm the one who dredged up all these painful emotions by talking about them in the first place. "Why'd you have to go and do that?"

In reply, I calmly inform them that although it appears that their loved one is getting worse, it is a clear sign that therapy may be working. Those dredged up emotions may be causing havoc in the household, but previously those emotions used to cause self-inflicted harm. Now they appear to be externalized rather than internalized. I often end with the admonition, "This, too, shall pass."

You see, the patient is most likely working through the emotions that they have suppressed for so very long. This means long days and nights, probably much discomfort and blame, and lots of hard work, but all for the right reasons. I am by no means telling you that you have to become severely depressed in order to heal. As a matter of fact, I would never bring a patient to a severe depression without providing them the proper coping skills to use between sessions!

You must keep in mind, however, that I refer to recovery from ED as a "systems approach." This means that the person with ED is not treated alone, in a vacuum, but surrounded by and part of their universal system. In other words, the entire family is the "patient." The entire family has to learn to cope with emotions and learn to communicate more effectively (more on communication in the next section).

Question: What do feelings and the flu have in common?
Answer: They're both contagious

That's right: feelings *can* become contagious if we're not vigilant. We may literally take on the feelings of others. You've probably experienced this yourself. Have you ever cried when your loved one was crying? Have you ever picked up on someone's enthusiasm? Has the bad mood of someone else infiltrated the room, bringing everyone else down? That's how easily your feelings can catch the emotional flu!

The more you learn to be in touch and comfortable with your own feelings, the less susceptible you will be to *catch* those of others, keeping you a more grounded individual. We have enough to worry about with our own emotions. How much harder do you think it will be if you're running around catching everybody else's?

Just consider my vocation: do you think it's easy to be a psychologist and watch and listen to the pain of my patients many hours a day? I'm by no means complaining, as I love my work, but a psychologist must be extremely grounded and stay emotionally objective in order to do this day in and day out, hour after hour, without a massive case of burn out. That means I've earned the right to help *you* learn to become a more grounded individual, too!

Emotional energy: simple versus complex feelings

Feelings give you energy. The more in touch you are with your feelings, the more you will be able to express them and the more energetic you will feel as a result. The freedom to express our emotions and to deal with them openly and honestly truly lightens our load and in turn frees us to place our energies elsewhere.

Sadly, the converse is also true: less energy can result when we are blocked to our feelings. The less you are in touch with your feelings, the more prone you will be to numb them with (or without) food or any other self-destructive activity.

There tend to be simple feelings and complex feelings. The simple, or basic, feelings include anger, sadness, grief, love, joy, and excitement, to name a few. The more complex feelings, such as eagerness, impatience, relief, and disappointment involve a combination of basic emotions and your thought processes.

Feelings come in mixtures. You may feel anger and love at the same time. Think of the holidays, for instance. This is a time when it's not only eggnog and rum getting mixed, but a variety of both painful and happy emotions at the same time. Perhaps seeing a certain family member results in a blend of both happiness to see him and sadness at the past hurts you two have shared. You enjoy the simple feeling of excitement upon seeing him, only to follow it up with a more complex emotion of severe disappointment.

It's not just people that get us to react; we can feel simple and complex emotions over a variety of other circumstances, such as the first day of school, making new friends, studying for a test, applying for a job, and many, many more. Again, these simple and complex emotions will never go away; we feel all day, every day. It's what we do with those emotions that determines the difference between health or distress.

How you deal with your emotions can often have disastrous or liberating results. Do you express your emotions freely? Or do your emotions get trampled underfoot? The difference can mean either health or more struggles with ED. If you have difficulty expressing them, you may behave in a way that is destructive rather than constructive. The expression "sorting out feelings" suggests the fact that you can feel several things at once, and it is normal.

Displacement: birthplace of the grown adolescent

Displacement—the act of blaming the wrong person for what ails you—plays a big part in keeping us from recovery. So often we target ourselves as the victim, via displacement, when it's an outside situation we're really upset about.

When you use bingeing, purging, or restricting as a way of avoiding your emotions, you are simply displacing your anger inward, onto yourself, rather than onto the target for which it was intended. More simply put, you are just not coping effectively with those strong emotions.

As you already know, this can cause more problems for you in the long run. Like tying your shoes or learning your ABC's, displacing emotions can quickly become habit. When we too often fall into the rut of displacing our anger inward, it becomes our emotional "default setting." That is where we go with those emotions, by default, each and every time. It's not the coach that upset us; it's us that we are upset with for being so fat, stupid, lazy, or *fill in the blank with what you think you've done wrong here.*

It's us; it's always us, so we displace that anger and learn to suppress our true emotions as a result. We don't convey them openly or honestly; we don't confront the friend or the adult or the situation. Instead we dwell on it, blaming ourselves, and swallowing our emotions along with our opportunities for good and positive health.

When the process of suppression begins in childhood, you tend to grow up being completely out of touch with your feelings, thus you begin to experience an emptiness that can spiral more and more into an eating dysfunction. Eventually, this spiral comes to a head, quietly but persistently becoming a full blown eating disorder later, or not so later, in life.

Unfortunately, when we become friends with ED, our emotional growth becomes stunted at that age! Yes! It's true. Since we stop developing emotionally, we get stuck in that stage. Finally, when we decide to get help to break up with ED, we have to relearn to feel again, or, in some cases, we have to learn to feel for the first time … as if we are at that very same age when we first met ED.

Think about it; you know it's true. You may be twenty years old today, but you and ED got together at age thirteen. Chronologically, you're age twenty, but emotionally you're still thirteen. As a result, you don't see the world as a normal twenty-something does, but as a new teenager would.

Despite the life lessons you might (or might not) have learned in those intervening seven years, you react as an adolescent, not an adult. How does an adolescent react to strong emotions? For the most part, not very well. Now perhaps you can see why ED therapy is so very, very challenging: not only do we have to deal with your issues with food, weight, body image, and the like, but we have to address the fact that you lost seven years in there somewhere and somehow get them back!

Warning: express yourself!

Madonna had it right when she said, "Express yourself!" Expression of our emotions, no matter how good or how bad, is the steam valve that lets us vent those damaging feelings before the pressure gets too high, too fast. What's the alternative? You guessed it: a blowout of massive proportions!

So be careful not to make yourself or anyone else "feel" wrong for simply feeling, no matter what the feeling. Too often we suppress our emotions out of politeness, respect, or duty. We don't reveal to our parents how we truly feel because we are supposed to be grateful for the roof, food, and clothing they provide us. We can't tell our friends how we feel or they might not like us.

Bull-hockey! *No one has the right to tell you* not *to feel.* Your emotions are yours and you have every right to them, whether they feel good or not. We cannot lose the negative ones and keep the positive. Just make sure that you are expressing feelings and not thoughts. Remember, your thoughts *can* be irrational (although everyone has the right to express his or her opinion), but your feelings just *are and they are valid!*

Feelings are not right or wrong. Never let anyone convince you that you should *not* be feeling a certain way. Maybe they just cannot understand your feelings, but that is their issue, not yours.

Others attempt to tell us to forget about it, or stop feeling that way, but maybe that's because *they* cannot deal with those emotions themselves or simply because *they* feel helpless when you are feeling so low. Contrary to what you might have been led to believe (usually by other people), you *cannot* control the emotions of others; you can only control your own.

There is a reason you are feeling a certain way, just as there is a reason they are feeling another. You are your top priority; to express yourself is to give voice to your identity, and those who truly respect and love you will find a way to deal with your emotions, one way or another. It may take time, but you will know those who are willing to assist you in the fight because they will be there, for better or worse.

Your *perceptions or judgments* that lead to those feelings can be valid or invalid. (Recall the previous chapter). It's the manner in which you *choose to express* those feelings that can cause problems, rather than the feelings themselves.

How am I feeling today?

Accepted	Contemptuous	Generous	Kind	Remorseful	Understood
Affectionate	Defeated	Glad	Lazy	Resentful	Uneasy
Afraid	Dejected	Good	Left out	Respected	Unfulfilled
Alive	Delighted	Great	Loved	Sad	Unique
Ambivalent	Dependent	Guilty	Loveable	Satisfied	Unsettled
Amused	Depressed	Grateful	Loving	Scared	Uptight
Angry	Desirable	Happy	Loyal	Secure	Used
Annoyed	Desperate	Hateful	Mad	Self-reliant	Useless
Anxious	Devastated	Helpless	Melancholy	Sexy	Valuable
Apprehensive	Disappointed	Honored	Miserable	Shy	Victimized
Ashamed	Discouraged	Hopeful	Misunderstood	Silly	Violated
Awkward	Disgusted	Hopeless	Muddled	Special	Vulnerable
Bad	Distraught	Horrible	Needy	Strong	Warm
Beautiful	Distrustful	Horrified	Nice	Stubborn	Weary
Betrayed	Eager	Hostile	Outraged	Stupid	Wishy/washy
Bitter	Elated	Humiliated	Overjoyed	Supportive	Witty
Bored	Embarrassed	Humorous	Overwhelmed	Sympathetic	Wonderful
Brave	Empty	Hurt	Panicky	Tender	Uncomfortable
Calm	Energetic	Ignored	Peaceful	Tense	Worn out
Capable	Enraged	Impatient	Pessimistic	Terrible	Worried
Caring	Envious	Inadequate	Phony	Terrified	Worthwhile
Cheerful	Excited	Inattentive	Playful	Thankful	Worthy
Cherished	Exhausted	Incompetent	Pleased	Threatened	Youthful
Childish	Fearful	Inferior	Pressured	Tired	Zealous
Comfortable	Forgiving	Inhibited	Preoccupied	Trapped	Zonked out
Concerned	Foolish	Insecure	Provoked	Touchy	Fill in Blank*
Confident	Frantic	Inspired	Put down	Troubled	Fill in Blank*
Confused	Friendly	Isolated	Put out	Trusted	Fill in Blank*
Content	Frustrated	Irritated	Regretful	Unappreciated	Fill in Blank*
Courageous	Fulfilled	Jealous	Rejected	Uncertain	Fill in Blank*
Curious	Furious	Joyful	Relaxed	Understanding	Fill in Blank*

By no means is this list exhaustive; there are as many emotions to feel as there are people to feel them. Use the blanks shown to fill in your own emotions. Don't worry; no one is peeking.

A call to action!

I am here to announce that you must allow yourself to go through the tough times in order to come out ahead of the game. If you suppress those feelings because they are uncomfortable or because someone tells you to do so, you will set yourself up for problems later on. Worse yet, your recovery will never effectively begin.

People find it so hard to quit drinking because the physical effects of withdrawing from their addiction to alcohol are simply too painful to continue much longer than a day or two.

I've seen people "quit" their emotions in much the same way. In fact, emotional pain can be much more severe than physical pain. An alcohol craving or caffeine withdrawal headache can last a few days or a few hours, respectively. The mental torture of feeling unwanted, unloved, or unnecessary can literally last a lifetime.

But I'm not asking you to quit anything; I'm asking you to give into those emotions you've been denying for so, so long. Think of it this way: "If you cannot feel it, you cannot heal it." The best way out of them is *not* to travel around them, suppress them, escape from them, or displace them; to overcome our negative emotions we must finally journey *through* them. Your sense of well-being and your physical health depend upon your willingness to acknowledge, identify, and express feelings at or near the time they occur in a constructive manner.

Recovery: it all starts with you

I know taking that first step toward emotional recovery is often the most difficult, most challenging step of all. What you need is a little motivation to get you going! One of the keys to motivating yourself is understanding your emotions.

Our emotions, to a large extent, drive our behavior. Not surprisingly, the desire for love, recognition, achievement, and meaning can all be powerful motivators. Knowing how to harness your emotional energy is the key to achieving a desired result in anything you set your mind to do!

Once you have been able to identify your feelings, it is very important to learn to express them. Expressing feelings is another term for letting them out.

It does not mean dumping them on somebody, or directing them toward the person you *perceive* to be responsible for how you are feeling. So often we equate emotional expression with an emotional outburst. Trust me, there are times when an outburst is warranted. However, there are several healthier ways of letting your emotions out than having a tantrum or stopping traffic with your road rage!

What is the alternative? What happens when you don't let your emotions out? What happens when you keep them bottled up, bubbling until the pressure builds and builds? When your feelings go unexpressed, they tend to be stored in your body as a form of tension or anxiety, which could lead to depression and a variety of other psychosomatic (mind-body) illnesses. (I bet some of you know just what I am talking about!)

Though they might stem from the brain (get it, brainstem?) these illnesses are far from imaginary. Anyone who has ever endured a severe tension headache or experienced a bleeding ulcer can tell you that the physical results of emotional turmoil are all too real!

There are several ways in which you can begin to vent your feelings. Remember, these are healthy suggestions for coping with your emotions. They are practical, use today/benefit today ideas for dealing with your feelings, but they are just a sampling. These may or may not work for you individually.

Unfortunately, there is no one activity that works for everyone all the time. I suggest you try each style to see which better suits your needs and, if you can't find one here, use the basic ingredients I've presented and concoct a recipe for healing of your own.

We are all different. Every one of us is special. That's what makes our healing unique, and what makes it so hard for writers of self-help to provide a magic umbrella under which all of us can fit! I offer solutions to help, and hope that you take them for what they are worth and adapt them for what feels right … for you!

Talk it out: give voice to your emotions (literally)

The first suggestion for coping with strong feelings is to "Talk it Out." There's no cute, subtle, or hidden meaning there; I mean, quite literally, to give voice to your emotions. Talk them out.

Sharing your feelings with a *supportive* friend, counselor, or significant other is a probably the most effective way in which to vent feelings. Sharing does not mean just talking about your feelings, as if you were an uninterested second party just relating an isolated incident, but actually letting your feelings out.

It is important that you have a high level of trust toward the person with whom you are sharing your feelings in order to be able to be as honest as possible. Further, this person you wish to share your feelings with should be someone who listens carefully *rather than* offering advice, opinions, or suggestions.

During your time of catharsis (cleansing of your soul, or Freud's famous "Talking Cure"), you need an active listener that will allow you to solve your own problems, rather than trying to enlist someone else to fix your problem for you. These are two very, very different things. For example, tell me how would it make you feel if you have a lousy day at school and your significant other tells you, "Then just quit!" Or, if you do not go to school, tell me how you would feel if you tell your partner what a terrible day it was with the kids and he says, "Then get rid of them." Neither option makes very much sense, does it?

I mean really, is it normal to go around quitting everything every time you have a bad day? I think not. And, seriously, is it really plausible to ignore or give away the children? I know this sounds ridiculous, but I want to make my point.

If my boyfriend responded that way it would make me more irate. It tells me that he just does not understand what I am feeling, nor does he care. It would seem to me that he just wants to "fix it" rather than help me get "through it."

My suggestion in such cases? Consider the source. The one thing we must keep in mind is that the people who want to fix our bad day may not exactly know how to express and deal with their own emotions. This type of quick-fix-it behavior could also indicate to me that they do not know what else to do besides try to appease us.

In my opinion, I think it would be better if he responded, "It sounds like you have had quite a day. I know how that feels. What can I do for you?" You see the difference? You do not have to feel pressured to quit or get rid of the kids. Here, your likely response would include, "Wow, he understands me." This is called reflective listening.

Now, I realize that this sounds totally idealistic for some of you in your current relationships, but think about how much nicer and healthier your relationships would be if only we *perceived* we were understood! (Remember: our perception is our reality.)

I actually suggest that if this sounds far-fetched to some of you, you sit down with your partner and share this information with him. When two people are coming from the same foundation, it is much easier to achieve peace in communicating thoughts and feelings! Give it a try. What have you got to lose (other than that mouthful of food)? Think about it. If you *felt* understood, you probably would not have to search for that comfort from ED. (I will discuss more on communication skills in the next chapter.)

In my experience, it is those individuals who have their own issues regarding difficulty expressing their own feelings that offer a fix-it solution. Or, again, maybe they feel so helpless seeing you suffering that they just want your pain to go away. We all know it does not work that way. Therefore, we have to teach our partners or family members or friends, or even co-workers, what we need in those moments of despair rather than becoming more frustrated.

Of course, not all of us are in a time, place, or relationship in which somebody else is willing, or even physically present, to listen to our fears, desires, hopes, and dreams. Then again, some of us may just not be ready to share all these intimacies just yet. Now, for those of you who do not have someone caring or empathetic to talk to, there are other ways to vent your feelings!

Discharging sadness: music to calm the savage beast

For many reasons, a lot of us were taught that we were weak if we cried. This is the furthest thing from the truth. Crying is a wonderful way to expel those strong feelings. Ever heard the expression, "You'll feel better after a good cry?" How could someone describe something that feels as horribly painful as crying as "good"? Well, anyone who's looked up from a face full of tears and seen the world anew knows exactly what that person meant!

Ask yourself the following questions: Do you ever cry? Under what circumstances do you cry? Do you cry because you feel lonely? Scared? Someone hurt you? Do you cry for no apparent reason? Do you only cry alone? Do you let others see you cry? Have you ever been on the verge of tears, and you feel like you would like to cry but are having trouble letting it out?

My suggestion when this occurs is to find an evocative piece of music that may have personal significance, or watch an emotional movie that will initially help to bring a vague sense of sadness to the surface. Have a box of tissues at the ready and then … let 'em flow! Far from being something to feel ashamed or embarrassed about, a good cry is as therapeutic as most things I could suggest at this juncture. Do not hold back. You deserve to cleanse your soul.

Of course, anything taken to extremes can have an adverse effect. For instance, if you have tried this and it makes you even sadder for a prolonged long period of time, then it is obviously *not* for you. However, many people say tears make them sadder, but in essence they just do not enjoy the pain of crying.

Crying is extremely therapeutic, and if you don't enjoy crying, I suspect you are worried about those broken records in your head, day in and day out, when you were younger (boys do not cry, be strong, do not be a baby, and so on). Talk to your therapist about this. Remember, if you can't feel it, you can't heal it! No giving up on me now!

Contrary to popular opinion (those broken records) crying is a sign of strength, not weakness. It means you are strong enough to show your emotions; you are brave enough to be seen as vulnerable and weak, even when both descriptions are far from the truth. Yes, guys, you too. Letting it out allows you to cope, move on, and feel a sense of calm.

While I recognize that this idea may not be for everybody, you must determine whether the pain and shame of crying is simply something you are trying to avoid or if crying truly is not the most effective tool for you. C'mon, be honest here! It's your recovery. Remember: Tears really *do* wash the windows of your soul!

Discharging your anger: let the floodgates open

If crying is a taboo for men, what do we ladies have? Well, anger … for one! You've heard the one about "the woman scorned." Well, unfortunately, many of us were taught by others that it is not "lady-like" to be angry. What they meant to say was that the manner in which you express your anger may not be lady-like.

You see, men and women were, unfortunately, socialized differently. For men it has always been acceptable to act out aggressively. Why do you think the prison system is loaded with more men than women? (I was also a forensic psychologist in Miami, Florida, so I actually do know what I'm talking about here!)

But the problem for women is multi-layered: if we do not learn how to get that anger out, we typically internalize, making our risk for depressive disorders actually two times higher than for men, and of course the statistics for befriending ED is ten times greater!

Anger can be a terrifying emotion, true, but it is normal and healthy, man or woman! It is quite possible to learn how to discharge your anger in ways that are not destructive. This does not infer dumping the anger onto someone else. Instead, your target should be an inanimate object. The following are helpful ways to vent angry feelings: hitting a pillow with both fists, screaming into a pillow, hitting a punching bag, or a vigorous workout (although be careful to avoid replacing your obsession for eating with an obsession for exercise, otherwise known as becoming an "exercise anorexic"). Personally, I use a heavy bag. (Yes, I get angry, especially when my patients end up in the ICU or ER in cardiac or renal failure.)

It really does help reduce the tension and helps me to cope with the rest of my responsibilities in a more efficient and effective manner! It may seem like a quick fix, but it actually alters our physiology; gotta love that healthy flood of endorphins pumping through our bloodstream. Once the anger and tension have subsided, we actually function in a less hostile, more relaxed, and less impulsive way.

These activities will allow you to unleash those compelling feelings and become a more productive and healthy member of society. Implementing new activities into your daily life will take some time. But, if you start now, they will become second nature sooner than later.

The last and final way to vent your feelings (and the most effective in my personal and professional opinion) is something I'm doing "write" now!

Write them out: journaling your way to good health!

If your feelings are running high and there is no one immediately available to talk to, then the next best way to cope is to use a "feelings journal." Far from being academic or "homework," this feelings journal is simply a piece of paper or a blank book (diary) where you write anything and everything you are thinking and feeling at the moment.

Journaling is no quick fix, but the cumulative effects of its process are amazing! Simply amazing! In the beginning, the mere act of writing out your feelings, versus waiting until your roommate gets home or your boyfriend answers his voicemail, will often suffice as an outlet until you have the opportunity to talk them out. However, used properly, the feelings journal will act as your confidant, allowing you to release those strong emotions at once rather than face the risk of having them build up and surface in a destructive manner or at the wrong or inappropriate time. A journal can be used for venting and therefore becomes an alternate behavior for bingeing, purging, or any other self-destructive behavior for that matter.

I've seen patients replace the urge to act out ED behaviors with journaling instead. In the same way that ED used to assuage their guilt, feed their soul, or validate their emotions, the journal becomes a safe haven, a harmless but helpful way to replace bad behaviors with good. At the very least, it will assist you in learning to see the connection between your thoughts, feelings, and patterns of behaviors that have plagued you for years.

Top ten benefits of journaling

Once the journal helps you to gain this insight, you will then be able to search for ways to change those old destructive patterns. So, here is a summary regarding the importance of journaling:

1. Journaling allows you to identify your feelings.

2. Journaling makes you more aware of your feelings.

3. Identifying an emotion puts a label on it, recognizing that the emotion actually exists. Awareness of an emotion means knowing exactly what the emotion is and how it makes you feel. Awareness takes identification of emotions and makes it personal.

4. Journaling helps you to clarify your feelings.

5. Journaling helps you to gain insight into your patterns of eating and how they are related to your emotions.

6. Journaling is a useful barrier against bingeing or overeating.

7. Journaling allows you to be honest. This is big! So many times we try to hide behind a façade when we are discussing our feelings with others. Maybe at times you are too worried that others will be critical of you, or maybe you feel you will become too vulnerable if you share too much.

8. Journaling provides freedom to express yourself!

9. Journaling prevents potential judgment and ridicule by others.

10. Journaling allows you to feel it so you can heal it!

Therapy in a notebook, psychology in a pen!

Clearly, journaling serves as a therapeutic intervention that can be done with little or no guidance at all. Hey, at the very least, it saves on a big therapy bill!

Many people tell me that they do not like writing or they just do not know "what to write." (I hear that one a lot!) I suggest that you write just that, "I have nothing to say. Why is Dr. Susie making me do this?"

That's a great start. If that's all you can write for the first day, fine.

Perhaps the next day you can try answering your own question: "I have nothing to say. Why is Dr. Susie making me do this? I guess because she says it will help. I don't know how. I mean ..." Typically, just priming the pump with a little internal Q & A is enough to really get those gushers of emotions, feelings, and buried experiences flowing!

But don't just take my word for it; let me help you get started: First, you can use any medium you choose: a notebook, a canvas (for painting), a diary, a scrapbook, or anything else you can think of. In the past, journals were drab, dull affairs. Today almost every bookstore, department store, stationary vendor, or gift shop has a variety of cool, funky, and fun journals, many of them featuring vibrant, artistic covers that actually invite you to open them up and be as equally artistic and creative inside!

Let your creative juices flow. If you are using a medium that you love to work with, you will find that you will be more enthusiastic about using it daily. The feeling of being an author, a painter, and so on, will allow you to feel good about doing this and it will eventually become a fun part of your daily existence.

This is an individual project. Anything that works for you will suffice. We are all different and require a variety of means to an end. So, feel free to write/draw/cut out anything that makes you feel better and brings out your unique qualities. The last thing I want to do is silence your creativity by placing harsh guidelines on this "assignment."

Use pictures, cut out things from a magazine, paint, color, draw, write poetry, or anything you can think of. Use as many colors as you can. Colors help to express how we feel. This helps with your creativity, because sometimes we find it difficult to put words to our feelings.

Once you begin writing and making it a part of your daily routine, you will be able to write more and your thoughts will flow freely! You *cannot* begin this activity thinking it is a cure-all. Nothing is a quick fix. It takes time to recognize the benefits of journaling, but believe me, it helps more than you could ever imagine if you give it time.

I think one of the biggest problems with journaling is that people want a tangible goal. This is intangible. We cannot necessarily *see* the progress. Just keep in mind that we are healing from the inside out. If you ask any of my patients, they all know that it's the healing from the inside that helps them deal with the outside!

Most importantly, you need to keep your journal where no one else can find it. This will help reduce your fear of others reading your personal information. As a result, this will allow you to write anything at all that you want, including thoughts, feelings, dreams, and aspirations you believe others might judge you for.

Remember what I said earlier in this very chapter: never let anyone tell you that your feelings are wrong, or that you shouldn't feel them. Journaling can be a great first step in hurdling past this belief.

I have one more note: if you are writing do *not* worry about sentence structure or grammar. It makes no difference if your sentences are run-ons or one word descriptions. This is for you and no one else to judge. Be easy on yourself and create anything you want.

A final rule for journaling is to keep it as close to you as possible so you have it when you feel the urge to binge, purge, or restrict, or when ED is simply messing with your mind. I strongly suggest that you use your journal at least before bedtime and when you awaken. This will help you remove those unwanted thoughts and feelings from your mind and allow you to sleep more soundly and to get your day off to a calm and peaceful start.

Letters to ED, to our bodies, to ourselves:

Dear ED,

I am not really sure what to say to you. I have such mixed feelings about you. One moment I am in love with you and the next moment I hate you. Grr, you have me so confused. I think that I am ready to be without you and I take the step and go and see people. But really I think you just set me up to come back.

You are so confusing. So instead of going and being like a normal happy person hanging out with my friends, you make me go there and have a miserable time. You remind me of how much better you are than my other friends. How much you have been there more than my other friends ... or so you tell me. You tell me that everyone in the room is better than me. Skinnier than I am. Smarter than I am. Everything about them is perfect. And everything about me is so wrong.

You make me depressed and make me feel like all I can do is turn to you. To come back and continue receiving the abuse that you already gave me through-

out our relationship. I chill with you for awhile, and I'm OK with that. Then after a while I see what is happening. I black out. I pass out. Something goes horribly wrong. And I realize that I need to get back on track.

So I try and do something good for myself once more and be healthy, but you are always there. You are like the stalker ex-boyfriend that would never leave me alone. The one who always wants me back, and I always come back because I'm comfortable with you. I don't know life without you. Life is scary because it is so unknown. But you are so scary because you kill me and tons of other people psychologically and some even physically.

I look at every other ED victim, and I think to myself why do they have an ED, they don't deserve it. They are such amazing people who can contribute so much to society. Why do you do this to us? Why do you make people so ill? People in the outside world don't understand you. They think that you are just a diet. I mean sure, I love throwing up. I am pissed when people say they can't be a bulimic because they hate to throw up and it's like, well, it's not my favorite thing to do either.

Why appear to the world as if we really aren't just sick? Why do we have celebrities say that there's an easy "cure" for this? That is more than bullshit! You really need to inform the world the hell that you put us through!

This is not a choice. This is a true disease. Why do you let people think that it's all about the weight? This just causes people to treat us like crazies. It's like yes, I have an eating disorder, and I might even be bipolar. But that does not make me any bit less of a functioning person than anyone else. That does not mean that I have to be treated like I have to be in a straight jacket at all times and that I am completely mentally unstable. I am a capable human being, for Christ's sake.

With lots of frustration,

"Janet"

CHAPTER 6

Communication Styles of the Happy and Healthy

Communication. We need it so much and do it so rarely. Communication. It's so healthy, and yet such a low priority. Between emails and memos and text messages and faxes and Blackberries, we can go an entire day, or even days, without talking to a single person. Of course, that still leaves good old ED for us to chat with, but we all know what *he* wants to talk about!

Communication is the key to unraveling the mysteries, anger, baggage, and emotions that contribute so heavily to eating disorders and the behaviors that cause them. In this chapter we will explore the differences and similarities between the five main types of communicating: 1.) aggressive, 2.) manipulative, 3.) passive, 4.) passive-aggressive, and 5.) assertive.

How can any one style of communicating, let alone five, affect what we eat or don't eat? Here is one such example: assertive behavior is just one of the many areas in which you can improve not only your body image, but your overall emotional, cognitive, and physical well-being, not only with ED but in your relationships with others. One can say that the key to understanding and overcoming ED is assertive behavior.

Learning how to say "no" to family, friends, and associates is similar to saying "no" to ED. Until you can assert yourself to family and friends, you will probably have difficulty saying no to ED. When you are not assertive and do not stand up for yourself, you get angry with yourself, feel awful, and turn to ED to feel better. ED seems to feel safe.

When you stand up to someone and express your own thoughts, opinions, needs, and desires, you will feel good about yourself and thus have no need to consult with ED. Hence, it may be easier to learn to say no to others before you say no to ED. Saying no to ED does not mean you do not eat; it means that you eat when you are physically hungry and not for emotional fulfillment; it means that you keep your food down, don't feel ashamed or guilty when you do eat, and never restrict your food because ED "told you to do so."

Think about the following: how many of you have trouble expressing yourself to your parents? Your friends? Your children? Your boss? Your spouse? Your co-workers? Many individuals with body image preoccupations are people pleasers, avoiding conflict and feeling too insecure to really state what they want or need.

So, for much of their lives, people pleasers have learned to either give in to others' requests in fear of being rejected, or they have harbored so much anger and resentment toward themselves and others that they have turned to ED as their only source of salvation to get through these situations. If you scroll through the examples above, you'll see that one unifying theme ties the message together: communication.

Too often, however, there is not so much communication as there is a communication gap. And guess who benefits the most when there is a gap in communication? That's right: our two-faced friend, ED.

ED and the communication gap: how assertiveness can bridge the gap!

Many people hear the word "assertive" and think it's a bad thing. We confuse assertion with aggression, aggression with violence, violence with danger, and danger with destruction. Following the links of that destructive chain, assertion often gets equated with destruction. But what if I were to tell you that assertiveness is actually the building block upon which you'll erect the foundation of your recovery?

Assertiveness is the simple act of taking back our lives. It is not unfair, unreasonable, or unjust. It is not rude, obnoxious, or boastful. It is merely reclaiming what is ours; it is merely reclaiming that which has been stolen from us.

Too often, however, it is our long-ingrained habit of pleasing people that robs us of our assertiveness. It is wonderful to please others; it is helpful and kind and wise and generous. However, we often forget to include ourselves among that list of people we must please.

Sometimes it's not even about pleasing others when we refuse to assert ourselves. Perhaps we are afraid: afraid of others not liking us, afraid of someone spreading rumors about how "selfish" we are, or afraid of what might happen if we wind up alone because we said "no" once too often.

No one can stay afraid forever; no one can please everybody. What I typically see in my people-pleasing clients is a lot of anger and resentment. We resent those we please for not caring about whether or not we're happy. We're angry at ourselves for forcing our own wants, needs, and desires down for the demands of others. What eventually happens when this anger and resentment builds up?

We feel powerless in the face of pleasing others. Where do we gain our power? ED is there; ED is always there, waiting to help us feel powerful and in control.

Instead of turning to our family, friends and mentors we turn to ED. And ED is the one who frightens us! He's the one causing this misery! How twisted is that? How bizarre that the one thing we fear the most is the one making all the rules?

Putting action into interaction

We will be talking a lot about communication in this chapter. Something else we'll be talking about is interaction. How you interact with others can certainly be a source of considerable stress in your life. Learning to become more assertive can reduce that stress by teaching you to stand up for your legitimate rights without hurting others' feelings or getting bullied yourself. This will also enhance your sense of self-esteem (the manner in which you judge yourself).

Some people believe that being assertive means being nasty or manipulating or complaining. This is the furthest thing from the truth! It is your right to express your desires, needs, thoughts, and feelings and not feel guilty about doing so. Still, I know this can be a big stumbling block for all of us people-pleasers.

Guilt is a huge factor in learning to be more assertive. We have to handle the guilt in a healthful manner and not just deny it. You can't just stop pleasing people cold turkey. You and I both know that's not how emotions work. You've probably been pleasing others all your life; I know I certainly have. Like most of what we've talked about here, becoming more assertive is a habit we must form one step at a time.

I am not suggesting that you shrug off other responsibilities or become lazy. It can feel good to help others; giving and being generous are both healthy behaviors (when they don't interfere with your own health and well being). What I am saying is that as you spend that time pleasing others, don't forget to please yourself. Once a day, and then more often as time goes on, take a break from all the people-pleasing and ask yourself these questions: Am I being served? Am I pleasing myself? Are my needs coming first?

It can be a colossal challenge for people-pleasers to put their needs first. Often we wait until the day is over and our energy's sapped before we finally pour that bubble bath or put on that favorite, empowering CD. By then I'm afraid it's too late. We need to start on ourselves first thing in the morning, not the last thing at night! Is that such a horrible thing? Putting our needs first? I no longer think so, but, of course, it took me years of practice, as well as a lifetime of introspection, before I could be assertive enough to even think about making my needs known.

Life doesn't happen in a bubble: the importance of interaction

OK, so, let's return to interaction. It is imperative that we interact with others. We are not an island. We are social creatures; there is simply no way to avoid it. Successful human interaction is not a fairy tale; it's entirely possible. The key is to interact in such a manner that you are neither Cinderella—running around attending to everyone else's needs—or the wicked stepmother—turning into a controlling, impossible-to-please shrew.

To be the most efficient and effective person you can be and still meet your needs is the path to your happy ending. We must learn to embrace ourselves again. Yes, I say again. As children we were our first concern. We thought as children do: me first, you second. Yes, a bit egocentric, of course, but we had no choice. We depended upon Mommy to take care of us. While this could oftentimes lead to selfishness and a lack of sharing, at least our hearts were in the right places.

As a child you may also have been taught to think, feel, and act in a certain way around adults. You may have heard messages such as, "Never cause conflict," "Never disagree with your elders," "Children are to be seen and not to be heard," "Your parents know best," and so on. Sometimes these messages are so strong and so loud that they echo even on into adulthood.

I'll never forget a dinner conversation I had with Sally's second husband. We were discussing cancer treatment, because he had just been diagnosed with the disease. I wasn't a child then. I was twenty years old. It just so happened that at the time I was working my undergrad internship at The University of Miami, Jackson Memorial Hospital, where we happened to be on the cutting edge of the latest cancer research. When I informed my grandfather of the new research, he argued with me.

It was a pivotal moment for me, for a variety of reasons. While I did not argue with my grandfather, I had accomplished a small milestone for myself: I asserted my newfound information instead of backing down. There was no need to argue; the evidence was what it was, and I wasn't going to back down on this topic. It was less a statement to my grandfather and more a testament to myself (to prove I could stand up and assert myself).

After dinner, my mother took me in the living room and told me *never* to talk back to an adult. And here I was thinking that, in my twenties, I was an adult. Silly me. What was I thinking?

Actually, I was thinking that *no one* would ever stifle me again. Of course, before no one could ever stifle me again I spent plenty of time stifling myself; it took years for me to learn that I was important enough to speak up again. So, in the meantime, I bottled it up and believed that I was a nobody. There were years of more negative self-talk and more feelings of worthlessness. So, where was ED when I needed him? Oh yeah, right there with me—again.

Remember: we always have to take a step back every now and again and examine our life as it relates to others. We don't do this to try and please them, but to try and understand them. So often what others say comes from their own upbringing and/or life experiences, and not from our own. The better we understand why someone else is saying something negative to or about us, the less damaging it becomes.

Particularly as adults, we have to understand what others tell us from their frame of reference. Some people are stuck in their cognitive schema (their old patterns of experience and ways of thinking) and they cannot seem to break the mold, hence they still look at us as children or refer to us as they remember us. They may not in actuality be talking about us when they comment negatively on our development or lack thereof.

Or they may be handing down old "lessons" that they learned, such as "respect your elders," that carry no weight in one specific instance. So, as adults *we have a choice*: stop the patterns and stop going back to ED.

While I strongly encourage you to reconnect with your assertive inner child, that is the only type of childish behavior I recommend at this time. As an adult, you have the option of deciding whether to continue behaving according to these assumptions that keep you from being an assertive adult or to finally think, feel, and behave as you desire, want, or need.

When you attempt to please everyone by putting their needs before yours, anger and resentment occur; you view yourself as being wronged. It's human nature. You please people long enough, eventually they'll start to expect to be pleased. You easily slip into those roles: people pleaser versus people "pleasee."

Over time you grow tired of your role, but the other person still expects the same treatment. Resentment builds up, feelings are hurt (yours, mostly), and you begin to feel betrayed by the people pleasee and by your own emotions. Then what happens? Go ahead; I think you know! ED kicks in! Yep, you guessed it. When you feel hurt, wronged, worthless, angry, resentful ... who knows best what you need? ED!

Well, don't you think it is time for a change? I also think it is time to stop feeling like a victim and start being a victor! Learning to cope more effectively with people and ED will ultimately help you feel more in control of your life. You will gain greater self-esteem and a greater sense of self-efficacy (the belief you have in your ability to succeed). The first place to begin is with assertive behaviors.

Getting a grip on assertive behaviors

Communication. Interaction. These two vital skills imply cooperation and a generous sense of give and take. Assertiveness, too, is a way of acting that strikes a balance between two extremes: aggressiveness and submissiveness. Assertiveness is an attitude and a way of acting in any situation where you need to express your feelings, ask for what you want, or say "no" to something you do not want.

To be assertive is to switch to a default setting in which *you* are the top priority. Many people confuse this with selfishness, while nothing could be further from the truth. In fact, the less honest we are with ourselves the less honest we are with each other. When we can honestly say that our needs have been met, then we are much more effective at assessing the needs of others, and then addressing them.

If you don't believe that assertiveness is the default setting for most people, simply look around. See the number of people who confidently and competently go about their day, not seeking power from food or feeling powerless at the altar of their warped body image. They are neither selfish nor entirely selfless; they are completely honest and healthily assertive. They know that to make others happy they must be happy themselves. The sooner we learn this lesson, the sooner we'll be on the road to recovery.

Becoming assertive involves self-awareness and knowing what you want. Behind this knowledge is the belief that you have the right to ask for what you want. Yes, I said you *do* have the right to ask for what you want. Now, say it with me: *I do have the right to ask for what I want.*

I want you to remember that word: right. We have treated ourselves as second-class citizens for too long now. Assertiveness means believing in your rights. It is just that simple, and just that difficult. We have been taught to believe that we are worthless. When evidence contrary to this belief magically appears—a kind word, a job promotion, a good grade, an approving glance from our partner—our self-talk quickly moves in to remind us of just how worthless we are.

Assertiveness is about taking back your right to be a first-class citizen. When you are assertive, you are conscious of your basic rights as a human being. Becoming assertive means you give yourself and your particular needs the same respect and dignity you would give to anyone else! Acting assertively is a way of developing self-respect and self-worth.

As you practice becoming more assertive, you should be familiar with the differing styles of communication. There are five basic interpersonal styles of communicating. I will first discuss each one, and later I will discuss ideas to help you interact in the most effective manner possible.

As you read the following descriptions of these basic communication styles, you may find that, depending upon the situation at hand, you fall into more than one category. This is normal, as we all interact differently in different situations. Pay attention to the following to determine how you react in certain situations. You will probably find that you respond more often in one way. What better time to be honest with yourself than in the privacy of your own company? It can only help you overcome your challenges—and kick ED *out* once and for all!

Of course, you will also gain insight into the manner in which your friends, family, boss, and co-workers interact. Gaining this insight will be helpful in order to not take interactions with others too personally.

I suggest if you have a significant other who is acting in any way besides assertively that you share this information with him/her so you can work together on communicating effectively. It is a great asset to have an open-minded partner to work with through these challenges.

Communication style #1: the Aggressor

The first style of communication is the *aggressive* style. This is behavior that includes accusing, threatening, fighting, and stepping on people without regard for their feelings. Aggression can result when assertion is taken too far; it is acting without regard for the feelings of others.

When you are aggressive, others will view you (with good reason) as demanding, obnoxious, attacking, abusive, insulting, and argumentative. Hence, no one prefers to be around an aggressive person. This is an inadequate way of escape that creates more pain and stress than it prevents.

The aggressive person is demanding, abrasive, and hostile with others; is insensitive to the rights and feelings of others; creates enemies and conflict along the way; and puts others on the defensive, leading them to withdraw or fight back rather than cooperate.

Many of us are familiar with both assertion and aggression, but just as many of us are unfamiliar with the difference between them. I have a simple test for telling the difference between aggression and assertion: if what you're asking for hurts, degrades, or embarrasses someone else, it's not healthy for either of you. It's aggression, not assertion.

Communication style #2: the Manipulator

The next style of communication is the *Manipulator*. Some people consider manipulation merely another part of the aggressive style. Although it is similar, it does have slight differences.

Chances are you know someone who is a manipulator. Manipulators are people who attempt to get what they want by making people feel sorry for them or guilty toward them. Instead of taking responsibility for meeting their own needs, they play the role of the victim or the martyr in an effort to get others to care for them; if it does not work they may become openly angry or feign (fake) indifference.

It's a symbiotic relationship. In other words, it takes two to tango. Manipulators can only be manipulative if there is actually someone to manipulate; otherwise they are left holding the bag for their own emotional needs. Unfortunately, manipulators are quite good at knowing who to manipulate. They can typically walk into a room full of people and know who they can dupe and who they can't. It's kind of like a predator ignoring the strongest prey and honing in on the weakest link.

Being manipulated is a miserable feeling; it causes mistrust, both in the manipulator and in you, for being manipulated. The person being manipulated may become angry and resentful toward the manipulator.

Those who lack assertiveness are often manipulated. It happens subtly. For example, someone who is manipulative might say something like, "Don't tell anybody, but if Ronald doesn't ask me to go to prom with him I might just have to swallow a bottle of my mom's sleeping pills. I mean, I just won't be able to go on ..." Clearly, this is someone seeking attention: a person wanting you to stop the presses, tell as many people as you can, and rush to her rescue.

Sadly, we are too often manipulated by ED. Don't believe me? See if this sounds familiar: "If my mom doesn't let me go to that concert, I'll just starve myself for the next three days" or "If my teacher doesn't give me an A on that paper I'll go eat everything in sight and puke it all up ..." If we're not careful, we can be manipulated by others as well as be manipulated by ourselves—or ED!

Communication style #3: the Passive-Aggressive

The next style is the *passive-aggressive* style. This style of communication includes those behaviors that do not openly express anger but serve the purpose of venting anger by "showing them" or "getting even." Here, unresolved issues and emotions go undetected and remain buried deep within yourself until such a point your behavior becomes maladaptive.

The problem with passive-aggressive behavior is that it does not allow the offender to know that he has offended. In addition, when using passive-aggressive behaviors it is unlikely that you will get what you want! An example of passive-aggressive communication is this: you are angry at your boyfriend, so you are perpetually late for a date.

The problem here is that your boyfriend probably does not even know you are offended and will only recognize your behavior as disrespectful. Think about it: Who is really winning here? No one! Basically, instead of asking or doing something that you really want, you perpetually complain or moan about what is lacking. As a result, you act by not acting. Instead of confronting your boyfriend about the real issue, you create mini-issues by not acting, by being late or lethargic or uncommunicative or asocial.

There's nothing overt about your behavior at the party—you don't make a pass at the bartender or wear a lampshade or go skinny-dipping—but by being late or acting indifferent you display a latent form of aggression that is harmful to both you and the person you are angry with.

People that act in this manner seldom get what they want, because they never get their true point across. Their behavior tends to leave people angry, confused, and resentful.

Communication style #4: the Passive

Another style of communicating is the *passive* style. Throughout my professional experience, I have found that many people with eating disorders interact in this unfortunate manner. Passive behavior is when you allow yourself to be pushed around, do not stand up for yourself, and you do what you are told regardless of how you feel about it. You are the ultimate doormat: a human punching bag. (Now, this is passive behavior to the max!)

While avoiding disagreements and conflicts, others will view you as cowardly, weak, fearful, victimized, intimidated, and easily used. "What's the big deal?" you say. "You're not hurting anybody," you say. Actually, the consequences of this behavior include being taken advantage of and storing up a heavy burden of anger and resentment that will no doubt result in ED behaviors sooner rather than later.

A passive or non-assertive person will yield to others' preferences while discounting her own rights and needs; not express her feelings or let others know what she wants; and make others remain ignorant of her feelings and wants.

Furthermore, a passive person will have feelings of guilt or the feeling that she is imposing when she does attempt to ask for what she wants. Someone who is passive will allow others to discount her feelings if she gives them the idea that she is not certain about what she wants; she is fearful that open expression of her needs will alienate her partner or even friends and family members.

Then, ED steps in to help you feel better about yourself, or so you think.

Many of us beat around the bush assuming others *should* know what we want. Never assume someone knows your wants, needs, dreams, or desires. When others do not conform to your vague requests it leaves you feeling rejected. It all goes back to our original discussion of communication in the chapter opener: you cannot expect someone to know what you want and need if you do not inform them.

This is a challenge for most people, particularly when we feel that what we have to say or even what we feel isn't important enough to share. How can we inform others about how we feel when we don't even believe we're worthy enough to feel in the first place? I often run into passivity in my private practice. People think everyone knows how they feel, which is impossible because they barely share how they feel with me, let alone their family and friends.

And yet it is not just the sufferer of ED who is passive; family members, friends, and partners are always surprised when their loved one doesn't know how much they are loved. Everyone thinks everyone else knows how they feel, yet no one is communicating. It can be very frustrating, particularly because the transition from being passive to assertive often feels like going from zero to sixty on foot!

Being passive may sound like the least harmful of these communication styles, but I point out that no style is more or less harmful than any other. Each has its weaknesses, and being passive is no different. Beating around the bush is counterproductive, and this counterproductiveness can lead to ED behaviors in order to stuff, purge, numb, and avoid your feelings of rejection, frustration, or a sense of severe self-*worthlessness!*

Communication style #5: the Assertive

How many of you found that you relate to any of these styles thus far? It's amazing, isn't it, to see ourselves portrayed so accurately? And yet that's what's so powerful: knowledge is your biggest weapon in the war against ED. The more you know about why you behave the way you behave, the more you can take away ED's power. He counts on you knowing less than he does; he counts on manipulating you.

Every word you read is another nail in ED's coffin. No matter how hard it is to change from being passive to assertive, or aggressive to less so, it must be done. If you could see how many late night phone calls I get from the emergency room as another ED patient is wheeled in, close to death, you'd know I mean it when I say this information truly *can* save your life!

It is wonderful to start understanding how others relate because you will feel less personally attacked. If you are still unsure as to the manner in which you communicate, go ahead and ask your significant other or a family member or a friend, and they will enlighten you!

Speaking of enlightenment, now for the most effective style of communication: the *assertive* style. When you behave assertively, you are able to express your true feelings, needs, and desires. You do not let others take advantage of you, and you stand up for your rights.

The advantage of behaving assertively is that you may actually get what you want without making others mad, hurt, or upset. (Remember my assertive versus aggressive test?) If you are assertive, you can act in your own best interest and not feel guilty or wrong about it. You can take back what is rightfully yours and give freely of yourself because your needs, wants, desires, and rights have been taken care of first (and not last, like in the old days)!

It won't just be you who benefits. Others will benefit by feeling more respected, too. In turn, others will ultimately show you more respect and view you as understanding, open, honest and direct, confident, strong, fair, and kind. While being an effective communicator, withdrawal and attack are no longer needed.

With assertive communication you are doing the following:

1.   Asking for what you want in a simple, direct, honest, fashion that does not negate, attack, or manipulate anyone else;

2.   Standing up for yourself without feeling guilty or apologizing;

3.   Taking responsibility for getting your own needs met in a way that perceives the dignity of other people;

4.   Allowing others to feel comfortable when you are assertive because they know where you stand;

5.   Making a simple, direct request instead of demanding or commanding.

Passive versus aggressive: a pop quiz

Before I continue with how to become more assertive, I want to give an example. Don't worry, it's a short pop quiz, but I think you'll see why I include it here when I'm done.

Question 1: You have lost thirty pounds in a very healthy manner and have been healthy and happy for the past two years. You and an old friend with whom you used to binge run into each other and make plans to get together after seven years of being separated. She brings lots of food and expects you to join her "for old time's sake." You indulge, because you do not want to make her feel bad. This type of behavior is considered what? (1) aggressive, (2) manipulative, (3) passive, (4) passive-aggressive, or (5) assertive.

Answer: Passive. You are giving in to someone else's needs—your friend's—and putting your needs down. Clearly, your friend should know better, and you could have celebrated your success healthfully, not painfully. But the choice was yours; you made the decision to join in. You acted passively, giving in instead of speaking up. The danger, of course, is that being passive and consuming all of that food, especially in the company of someone you already have baggage/issues with, may trigger a relapse. Perhaps later you go home and purge; or maybe you restrict for the next several days; or maybe you drift back into a world of depression and self-loathing.

Question 2: OK, now let's consider the same scenario. What would happen if you tell your friend with all the food, "I am not going to do that! I grew up and got over that. I cannot believe you are still doing it! How disgusting! I can't believe how weak you are!"

Answer: Aggressive. Your aggression results in an outburst from you and probably causes a lot of hurt feelings for your friend. Remember the difference between assertion and aggression? When you're assertive, nobody gets hurt. When you're aggressive, the person you were aggressive to and you both get hurt. It's the ultimate lose-lose situation!

How to turn this very same situation into a win-win? Let's try using your assertiveness in a positive manner. In this scenario, you could gently explain to your friend how wonderful you feel in your new way of coping with things and how you'd like to share some new experiences with her. Perhaps you can gently guide her away from the negative, ED-like behavior and steer her toward some more positive alternatives that you've learned in books like this one and in your own personal therapy. This would be a win-win situation for both of you, huh?

OK, speaking of "food," are you ready for some food for thought? Now it's time for us to get busy; it's time for you and me to begin discussing what it takes to be more assertive, why it's so important, and where to begin.

Let me give you a fair warning: learning to be assertive takes time, patience, and practice. Practice makes proficient ... not perfection! (Uh, there's no such thing as perfection, by the way!) If you are accustomed to being passive, aggressive, manipulative, or passive-aggressive in your requests, you must learn one step at a time. The following are rules for asking for what you deserve, desire, and need, as you deal with this new sense of assertiveness.

Rules for living an assertive lifestyle

We begin with a formula. In order to assert yourself, you must keep this format in mind: I think (perception or understanding); I feel ("I" messages); and I want (the actual desired event). I know; it's hard to see a formula without the proper perspective. Abstract formulas matter little if we can't apply them to something concrete. So let's try a little real-life example on for size, shall we?

Let's apply it to a situation: I think that I'm a valuable employee who has been with the company long enough to rate; I feel like my work here is undervalued; I want a raise. See how the formula works? Assertion starts as a thought: I think that I'm a valuable employee who has been with the company long enough to rate.

It evolves into a feeling: I feel like my work here is undervalued.

It results in a desire: I want a raise.

All that's missing is an action!

Action, as we all know, does not happen overnight or without effort. We must take action to make action. In order to live assertively we must practice constantly. As children we asked for what we wanted naturally, whether it was reasonable or not. Instead of teaching us to make reasonable requests, more often than not others simply told us to make no requests at all. After years and years of having this drummed into us, most of our assertion was drummed out!

Assertion is a habit; we must take actions to assure that we practice good habits and don't fall back into old habits. It's not always easy, but the following rules should be helpful for avoiding such slips:

- **First, agree on a time and place that is convenient for you and the person of whom you are making a request.** Let's say you're asking your boss about that raise. You want to meet at a time and place where you can both be comfortable.

- **Make sure your requests are clear, direct, and non-judgmental.** Don't go into the meeting preparing to attack. This is a very specific discussion about your job performance, your expectations, and your value as an employee. Do not make it about how the company is sexist, men are treated better, or how everyone in your life has always treated you this way. Be specific, be clear, and be reasonable.

- **Speak clearly, audibly, and firmly.** Speak politely, broach the subject, outline your rationale, and then make your request.

- **Keep your tone of voice moderate.** Do not demand "I want a raise!" at the top of your lungs the minute you walk into the room. There is a time, and a tone, for every situation.

- **Keep the request small enough to avoid major resistance.** Do not ask that your salary be made competitive with the new CEO. Research what other employees in your position make and adjust your request accordingly.

- **Keep the request simple and understandable.** Cut the "fat" from your argument. Don't go on and on about your qualifications; you'll only oversell yourself. Make it as simple as possible. In this case, less is more.

- **Do not blame or attack.** Your boss is not the enemy. Remember, this is not about sexism, politics, the girl in the next cubicle over, or the guy that's your boss. This is about you, your value, and your pay increase.

- **Be objective.** Look at the situation from your employer's point of view. Listen to his explanation and examine it from all angles. There is generally room for growth on both sides of the negotiation table.

- **Be specific.** Don't make unreasonable demands or leave the option open for the company to determine the figure. Say something specific, such as, "After evaluating my time and performance with the company I would like to request a 5 percent increase in pay."

- **Describe your wants in terms of behaviors, not attitudes.** Talk about what you've done, not how great you are. It's results that matter, not assumptions.

- **Stick to the facts.** Again, this is about you, not your co-workers, boyfriend, your accumulating bills, or, for heaven's sake, your mother! You want a raise and here are the reasons why, period.

- **Maintain eye contact.** Assertion begins in the eyes and moves downward. You can't assert yourself if you can't express yourself through eye contact.

- **Do not look down or away from the other person.** Stand or sit erect with your head up.

- **Keep arms and legs uncrossed.** Crossing them puts others on the defensive. Yes, body language says it all!

- ***Do not* apologize after you have made your request.** This negates your entire request. It detracts from your message and may renew your doubts about your right to speak on your own behalf. Saying "I'm sorry" is ED's way of telling you you're wrong, stupid, worthless, and bad. ED is not going to win this time!

- **Practice making your request so that it feels more comfortable.** Rehearsal is key! Repetition is the key to success. The more you do something, the more second nature it becomes! Practice makes *proficient.*

- **Focus on the results.** Mention the benefits of getting your needs met rather than the disadvantages of denying your request. This will keep it in a positive light and will not appear as if you are being manipulative.

- **Use "I" messages that express your feelings without blaming others.** Rather than saying, "You make me angry because you pay me so little," the "I" message would be, "I *feel* insulted because I don't make what I should." This gives you personal power. And remember, no one can tell you your feelings are wrong!

- **Connect the feeling statement to the behavior of others, rather than to the person.** Say something specific if things go poorly, such as "I feel insulted or disrespected when you counter with 2 percent instead of the 5 percent I asked for," rather than, "I feel angry because you are inconsiderate." This will only put the other person on the defensive, causing a multitude of secondary problems. Rather, state your feeling about their behavior. Remember, feelings are not wrong. They just are! No one can debate your feelings!

- **Get rid of the impossible expectations of yourself.** You do not have to be perfect in everything you say or do. Actually, you *cannot* be perfect. There's no such thing!

- **Be confident!** Abandon your thoughts of, "I am not good enough" or "I am not as important as others."

Stumbling blocks on the way to assertion

We all know that rules are made to be broken. (Even I break them sometimes!) Still, without rules there would be anarchy, and you know ED would just love that. However, we are going to try to stick to the rules for being more assertive, even though we all know there will be stumbling blocks along the way. These stumbling blocks, in my experience, most often have to do with communication.

I know that it's not easy to change our stripes, but we must try. The alternative is to let ED win, and, although I'm not a competitive person, I just can't do that! So, to persevere we must learn to communicate. This often means starting with yourself. When you are trying to be assertive, you must take baby steps. If you're like most ED sufferers, you've been a people pleaser far too long to simply quit cold turkey and expect people to accept the changes at face value.

At first, you can expect a fair number of conflicts. Let's say your boyfriend is used to you driving him around. Well, he's got a perfectly good car with low mileage. Why can't he drive? Actually, that's a pretty good argument. When he complains about having to drive, you might say, "You have a perfectly good car with low mileage. It would make me happy if you would drive sometime."

Remember our rules and *be specific*! You have to be assertive on a case-by-case basis with the individuals who stands in the way of your own wants, needs, and desires. You want to have less mileage on your car, and it's not fair that you and your boyfriend can't share the driving. That is the argument, *not* the four thousand other things he does to make you angry. Assert yourself one issue at a time. To let it all pile up and rush out is only to shoot yourself in the foot.

Likewise, don't take your issues with your boyfriend out on anyone but your boyfriend. If you have an issue with him, settle it with him. After all, he is the only one who can solve the problem. Your mom can't, nor can your brother, nor your English teacher.

A lot of times we invite audience participation when we assert ourselves. We fear confrontation, so we avoid private conversations. We think our boyfriend won't blow up at us if we're at the family dinner table, surrounded by loved ones or friends. But when an audience is present, you invite people to take sides. Some will agree with you, others with him. Neither side will "win" because nothing will get accomplished until the two of you talk it out alone. Besides, it's just not fair to bring other people into it; it isn't fair to the other people or to your boyfriend!

Don't rush being assertive. Time is the great equalizer. You will need time to grow in your assertiveness. Others will need time to deal with you being more assertive! Give them that time. Maybe you have five issues you'd like resolved with your boyfriend. Do you have to solve them all today? Don't even try!

There is no scoreboard for assertiveness; you have all the time in the world to get healthy. In fact, the longer you take to learn and become proficient, the more lasting the effects. Tackle the "equal driving" issue to your satisfaction and then step back; don't race in to tackle another issue, and then another. Too much of a good thing can often turn sour. Simply assess what you did right and what you did wrong and apply what you learned to another issue when the time feels right.

Whatever you do, don't get greedy. You will be amazed by how some people react to your newfound assertiveness. Take your boyfriend, for instance. He might not even give up a fight. He might see the logic of your "equal driving" argument and smack his forehead and say something like, "Why didn't you ever mention it before?" Suddenly, he's driving all over the place, making up for lost time, and you naturally soak it up like a sponge.

But wasn't your argument for "equal driving?" If you allow your assertion ("Let's both drive every other time") to become aggression ("You drive, *all* the time"), you haven't healed at all; you're simply exchanging one form of communication—passivity—for another—aggression. You might as well be hopping out of the frying pan and into the fire!

Respect is at the heart of any assertion. Respect for yourself and respect for the other person. You are not asserting yourself to hurt someone else; you are asserting yourself to heal yourself and to respect others at the same time. When you cross the line to disrespect, you are doing more harm than good to both of you!

Remember to assert yourself as it pertains to a specific situation. We talked earlier about how long those of us with ED have been people-pleasers. Our tendency when finally asserting ourselves at a date later in life is to make up for lost time; we may focus on one specific issue as a way to funnel all of our past hurts and transgressions.

For instance, asking your boyfriend to drive to a movie is *not* the time to use words like "always" and "never." These are absolutes and life encompasses shades of gray. The statements may be true—you *always* drive and he *never* does—but such absolutes focus on the past. Your target is the here and now and preparation for the future; always remember that!

The bottom line when asserting yourself is to *be specific.* If you can remember those two little words you will be off to a great start. Your request to get your boyfriend to drive more often was a great one; it was specific, to the point, targeted, and on task. And it worked! Now he's driving so often you have to physically pry the keys away from him to get a turn!

But what might have happened if your request was a tad less specific. Let's say, for instance, instead of asking for something specific like "less driving" you requested "more respect." That is a great goal, but how is it achieved? More respect could mean a variety of things to a guilty boyfriend: putting the seat down, bringing you flowers, driving more, or not telling you to "calm down." Respect means different things to different people. It's far too broad a term! What you requested in regards to the car was so specific and so successful that it actually achieved your greater goal of "more respect." See how that works?

The case for being specific

Being specific is ground zero for asserting yourself. For example, be more specific than just telling your partner, "I want to lose weight." Explain to him a bit more, such as why it is important to you. Saying, "I want to lose twenty-five pounds" to someone who loves you just the way you currently are will make it difficult for them to support you.

However, if you are more specific and instead say, "I want to lose weight because I feel uncomfortable in my clothes and I want to prevent health problems," the other person will most likely gain a better understanding and will likely be more supportive of your efforts (unless, of course, you are suffering from a distorted body image). Expressing your thoughts and feelings will help to clarify the situation for the listener while helping the listener develop more empathy and be more attentive to your requests. When expressing feelings, you must learn to use "I" statements. (We've talked about those throughout this chapter.) These "I" statements will allow you to have personal power rather than blaming someone else for your lack of something.

Of course, the other person may still hear what they want to hear or try to argue with you about your feelings, but once they get used to you taking that power and expressing your feelings rather than being on the attack, they'll start to adjust. Just because you change doesn't mean the other person will change immediately. It takes time for everyone to adjust to the new you!

As another example, rather than say, "You are inconsiderate when you come home late," it is more effective to say, "I feel disrespected when you come home late." This makes the statement less attacking and critical, and thus allows the offender to respond without needing to be defensive. And remember, your feelings can't be wrong! They simply are.

I strongly encourage you to sit down with your partner, friend, or family member and discuss these techniques. Remember, this is a systems approach; I teach this to all of the families I work with so they are on the same page and understand the independence that their son or daughter needs to gain or regain from ED and from the family in order to conquer this illness. If both/all of you are working on these ideas together, there will be more understanding and patience while the changes are taking place.

Knowledge is power if you apply that knowledge. Do not keep your partner, family, or friend in the dark about your efforts to change—inform them.

Your bill of human rights

The following is a list of rights that we all have as human beings. These rights will help to remind you that you can be assertive and you do not have to carry around that burden of anger and resentment.

Memorize them, live them, and love them. If it helps, post them on your fridge for the entire family to learn, internalize, and apply; read them in the morning, afternoon and evening; bite them, chew them, swallow them … digest them!

Let me preface this list by stating that this is not to be taken in an extreme or concrete manner. Take each declaration seriously, but generally!

If you just remember and apply these phrases, not only to yourself but to others as well, you will be able to cope with more responsibility than you ever dreamed of! You must take care of your needs before you can be effective in caring for all of your other responsibilities! Let's get ED out of our lives once and for all!

Finally, while perusing this Bill of Human Rights, I urge you to reflect on the original Bill of Rights. You know? The one that says, "All men (and women) are created equal." That's right; you deserve to be pleased just as much as the people you've been pleasing for years deserve to be pleased:

- I have the right to ask for what I want.

- I have the right to say no to requests or demands that I cannot meet.

- I have the right to express all of my feelings, positive or negative.

- I have the right to change my mind.

- I have the right to make mistakes and to not have to be perfect.

- I have the right to follow my own values and standards.

- I have the right to say no to anything when I feel I am not ready, it is unsafe, or it violates my values.

- I have the right to determine my own priorities.

- I have the right to expect honesty from others.

- I have the right to be uniquely myself.
- I have the right to be angry at someone I love.
- I have the right to feel scared and say I am afraid.
- I have the right to say I do not know.
- I have the right *not* to give excuses or reasons for my behavior.
- I have the right to make decisions based on my feelings.
- I have the right to my own needs for personal space and time.
- I have the right to be playful and frivolous.
- I have the right to be healthier than those around me.
- I have the right to be in a non-abusive environment.
- I have the right to make friends and be comfortable around people.
- I have the right to change and grow.
- I have the right to have my needs and wants respected by others.
- I have the right to be treated with dignity and respect.
- I have the right to be happy.

Translating your rights into your actions

We all have rights. Your ultimate right is to be the sole judge of yourself and to initiate and accept the consequences of your own actions, your own thoughts, and your own feelings. Remember, others have these rights as well. So, when they are standing up for their rights, they deserve respect too!

This chapter is *not* about disrespecting, ignoring, or lording over others. It is about respecting yourself. I am not urging you to cross the line from being passive to being selfish! I am simply suggesting that you learn to find time for yourself every day. Balance is the key to successful and healthy living. Finding time to nurture yourself will make you that much more effective in caring for your loved ones! That is precisely why you have to learn to let others know when you need your time for you.

After all, if you are exhausted and run down due to the fact that you have not learned to say "no," how in the world do you think you will find the energy to care for everyone else? One thing to remember: when you are standing up for your rights, you must make sure you are doing it in a safe environment. Use your social judgment!

Finally, being assertive does not mean that you will get what you want. It will simply allow you to get your opinions, needs, desires, ideas, thoughts, and feelings off your chest. And who knows? You may actually get your needs and desires met and get your point across after all, while enhancing your overall health and emotional well-being at the same time! Imagine that!

An open letter to ED

Remaining passive keeps ED alive! Remaining angry keeps ED alive. Asserting yourself will keep ED away! You tell him! Kick him to the curb! He's not welcome here anymore! In fact, as we end our discussion regarding the various types of communication, I'll include a message you can use to send ED on his way, for once and for all:

Dear ED,

Now that I understand the basic types of communication—the good, the bad, and the ugly—I have a message for you: you are no longer welcome here. In asserting myself, I am saying good-bye to you. I know that you won't go away immediately, or even easily. But if I don't take the first step now, while these forms of communication are fresh on my tongue, when will I ever?

I must begin to assert myself. I can't do that with you whispering in my ear, tugging on my sleeve, or nipping at my heels. Good-bye, ED. You've manipulated my passive self for the last time.

Sincerely,

Ms. Assertive!

Putting it all together

I hope I've "communicated" the various styles of communication properly. If so, it will be easier to see just why it is so important to disengage yourself from passive, manipulative, aggressive, and passive-aggressive behavior. Despite their differences, all of these types of communication have one thing in common: they make it easier and easier for ED to communicate with us!

Only the last style of communication—assertiveness—can lead to our salvation. It might be easier to be passive, it might feel better to be passive-aggressive, you might get more done being manipulative, and you might even get rid of a few negative emotions by being aggressive, but no style of communication can lead you to health like asserting your own needs in a rational, specific, and healthy manner.

We seek ED out to feel powerful. Communicating effectively can give you that power, with or without ED. So why do we need him anymore? When you communicate effectively you eliminate the need to seek power elsewhere. Your needs and desires are made known and actualized. When that happens, you feel better, embrace a stronger attitude of self-confidence, and are better able to face your demons in healthy, positive ways.

ED counts on you communicating poorly. He is stronger when you get emotional, tongue-tied, embarrassed, or boastful. By being specific and reasonable you can assert your own needs properly and effectively. You are important, you are worthwhile, and you are one step closer to recovery. All it takes is believing in yourself.

All it takes is asserting yourself …

Letters to ED, to our bodies, to ourselves:

Dear ED,

Life with you is truly a living hell! You entered my body and mind eight long years ago and your power over me has grown to where I don't even know myself anymore. I have completely lost all self-worth because you have forced me to believe that I have no qualities worth liking. I despise you and wish for your death!

Over the years my mind has been twisted to accommodate you. I have listened and believed everything that you have ever told me: "Your thighs touch so you need to increase your workout. You ate too much so you need to purge. She's thinner than you so you need to starve yourself."

But what has this ever fucking gotten me? I'll tell you what: misery, self-hatred, distorted images, embarrassment, fear, and so many more ugly qualities. You always promised me happiness if I followed your way, but you have brought me nothing but grief and un-happiness.

Along the way I always thought that maybe you would one day be right. That maybe I could be what you wanted me to be. But I have realized that no matter what I do you will never be satisfied. I will never be perfect!

You have led me to believe that it is OK to abuse my body. So I listened. And I hurt my body day after day, just to please you. Just to be perfect. You caused me to be the abuser, ED—while my body withheld this perfection every single day.

You have turned me into something that I would never want to be. Something that I would never accept from anyone else. I can no longer let my body be the object of your destruction. It and I have suffered for way too long. Your control needs to be taken, and it's time I take it from you. I hate you and everything you say to me. I hate the way you make me feel; and worse, I hate the way you make me behave. For the sake of my body, I want you out of my life. I know that you won't just leave, but I will continue to fight everyday. So I'll say it now, because I'll mean it one day: Good-bye Ed!

Unhappily yours,

"Sharon"

CHAPTER 7

Shot Through the Heart

(And ED's To Blame)

OK, gang, time for a little Q & A.

Question(s): Why do we act the way we do? Why do we continue to restrict or binge/purge when we know it's killing us? Why does it take years and years of therapy to overcome our eating disorders? Where are eating disorders born in the first place?

Answer: Triggers.

A big part of *why we do what we do* is because we don't take the time to explore why *we did what we did.* (Confused yet?) Think about it: if you were to analyze some of your most painful moments, or the times when you sought the most personal power or validation through acting out with ED behaviors, no doubt you could accurately pinpoint the specific triggers that resulted in those behaviors.

Triggers are just that: verbal, physical, or situational sparks. However, instead of sending a bullet speeding toward a target, they ignite something even more damaging: an unpleasant or even dangerous behavior that sends us reeling, whimpering and vulnerable, into the arms of our old friend ED.

Like moving targets, we are *all* vulnerable to these individual triggers. Even after recovery, and sometimes years after recovery, we still find ourselves trembling at the sudden appearance or introduction of one trigger or another.

However, we can be proactive in diminishing our vulnerability. In this chapter we will do our best to understand triggers and, more importantly, how to defend ourselves against them with the only weapon we have available to us: preparation.

The root of all triggers

A trigger is defined as "stimuli that initiates or precipitates a reaction" (Webster's Unabridged Dictionary, 1989).

Triggers are at the root of most of our ED behaviors. What causes triggers? Where do they come from? Triggers can be caused by people, places, and things/situations. So much of what we have talked about so far in this book has built up to this point (you'll often hear me referring back to previous chapters during this one), because now we can finally understand why these triggers set us off.

The worst thing about triggers is that they can happen anytime, anyplace; and we respond to them so poorly. That's because, for the most part, we're unprepared to deal with them.

Triggers are everywhere, lurking just out of sight, waiting for us to stumble across them. Turn this corner and there's a trigger; turn another corner and there are two more triggers tag-teaming us. The more we give into them, the more triggers we find. The less we prepare to defend ourselves against them, the more damage these triggers can do.

Therefore, the gun metaphor is a good one. Triggers send emotional firepower in our direction and, like those paper targets hanging in the breeze, we are defenseless to do anything about them. They assail us with no rhyme or reason; they attack us at the most unexpected time.

Here are a few great examples of some not-so-great triggers:

- *People:* The relative who shows up at Thanksgiving and starts right in on the "backhanded compliments," telling you how much you've "grown" with a wink, nicknaming you "Slim" because it's "just so funny when you call someone the opposite of what they are." Merely by appearing at your front door, this person triggers a torrent of unpleasant responses that, more often than not, result in even more unpleasant ED behaviors.

- *Places:* The gym can be a building-size emotional trigger that does more damage than it does good. Here is a place we are drawn to, a source of power and control over ED, and yet to see so many beautiful men and women living such healthy lives can often send us spiraling back through the negative experiences we had growing up.

- *Things:* Yogurt! Need I say anymore? Inanimate objects are powerless until we give them emotional significance, and yet look at how often a simple "thing" like yogurt, donuts, sweatpants, or glossy fashion magazines full of skin-and-bone models can set us off in an emotionally damaging tailspin.

- *Situations:* Social situations can be huge triggers. Take, for instance, the employee get-together where you are supposed to strike just the right blend between perky and professional, or friendly but not too friendly. These high wire acts can often send us reeling, thinking back to our high school cafeteria or recess/playground adventures in which we tried to act like insiders, even though all along we felt like outsiders.

The five types of triggers

Do any of these people, places, situations, or things sound even remotely familiar? I'm guessing so. Actually, we should be familiar with most, if not all, of the common sources of triggers. Why? Some of the most common triggers are things that we have discussed thus far in this book.

There are five root causes for our emotional responses to triggers (and we've already discussed most of them). Let's recap:

- Trigger #1: *Emotions*
- Trigger #2: *Stress*
- Trigger #3: *Self-talk*
- Trigger #4: *Social Pressures—People*
- Trigger #5: *Environmental Cues*

Trigger #1:
Emotions

Yes, all emotions, both positive and negative, trigger our behavior responses. That is because for every action there is a reaction; for every cause there is an effect. Emotions are the gasoline fueling our personal gas tank.

They drive us to be happy, sad, productive, or depressed. They fuel our every day, from sunup to sundown, providing us with no end of emotional triggers to contend with. It is important to remember that all emotions are healthy. Feelings come from somewhere inside us; to suppress them is to deny them. We simply have to learn how to identify them, express them, process them, and manage them. Suppressing them will cause ED to be with us forever, but managing them will kick ED out ...

Here is how our emotions trigger our responses:

Positive emotions:

Even when we feel on top of the world, we may treat ourselves with a dinner on the town (overeating or a binge) to celebrate, which may lead, for some of us, to an inevitable purge, or may then lead to a day or two of restricting.

How does this happen? How can we self-destruct and engage in negative behaviors even when we feel good? The explanation is fairly simple, though how we act is complicated. When our brain chemistry causes us to feel good, it inhibits our negative thinking, making us feel almost invincible; that second helping of cheesecake doesn't matter (at the moment) because it is well-deserved in honor of our celebration.

Positive emotions are to be enjoyed; we should not fear them. However, as with most of the emotions in this chapter, it is how we choose to deal with them that could make us vulnerable to ED.

Negative emotions:

Using food (bingeing, purging, or restricting) as comfort to numb painful or uncomfortable feelings is a way that many of us cope with our negative emotions. (This is another trigger that we have discussed in chapter four.)

Negative emotions are doubly dangerous because, unlike external triggers, they lurk beneath the surface, always there, ready to do damage at a moment's notice. I can clearly remember a time in my life when, during college, I had a rare open afternoon every so often. I'd sit in a movie theater, blissfully unaware of the real world for a movie or two, but just about half an hour before the movie was over a wave of sadness would wash over me.

There was no reason for it; I wasn't going anywhere unpleasant or experiencing anything but relaxation, but it was those negative emotions creeping in because, once the movie was over, I'd be back to reality.

Has this ever happened to you?

Trigger #2:
Stress

This is a big trigger! However, many of you mistakenly think that all stress is bad. Stress is actually an important part of life. Without it we'd all be sedentary. Like emotions that can be both negative and positive, we need a moderate level of stress in order to get things done.

We hear a lot in the popular media and from TV doctors about how to avoid stress, beat stress, or even eliminate stress. Frankly, this is bad advice. The key is not to eliminate stress completely, but to learn to *manage* stress. (But that's a whole other book.) Stress should be a part of our daily lives: it gets us out of bed and makes us get dressed and go out and face the world. Unfortunately, high levels of stress can also send us spiraling into the waiting arms of ED.

My point here is that stress *can* be a trigger for ED behaviors to arise if we haven't learned to manage stress effectively. Whether it's good stress or bad, our body's physiological system still responds in the same manner. It must adjust to the *change*. The adjustment our bodies must undergo must be managed effectively for us to cope without ED getting involved. Therefore, learning to manage stress is one coping skill that you and your therapist must take on when working through your journey toward recovering from ED!

Trigger #3:
Self-talk

Hmm, heard of *this* somewhere before? Yep, your very own self-talk is a big, huge trigger to your ED behaviors. Your self-talk can make or break your day, your week, your month, and your life! Remember? Your self-talk, your perceptions, your life! Since you have control over it, use it to your advantage!

Trigger #4:
Social Pressures—People

Feeling obligated to another person is another big trigger. Obligation will get you every time. ED sure loves it when you feel obligated! Let's say your aunt has you over for Thanksgiving dinner. She says, "I spent all day baking your favorite pie. Remember how much you loved this when you were a kid?" Ever heard of a guilt trip? Talk about an "obligation trip!" I'll bet you would feel obligated to eat it, wouldn't you? So, what happens? You eat it. You feel like crap. ED is screaming at you, "You fat pig ... how could you have eaten that? Now go puke before you get huge." That sounds like something ED would say, right?

How can you possibly avoid feeling so obligated? I mean, come on, this is your dear old aunt. Right? Well, like I've said a hundred times over: you can't control your feelings; you can only control the manner in which you choose to respond to them. You may feel obligated, so what you *can* do is deal with your feelings of obligation differently. Two words there sum up this section superbly: *deal differently.*

In chapter seven we discussed assertiveness in depth. If you need to, revisit this section and think how acting assertively might have helped you cope with this situation. For instance, instead of succumbing and eating sixteen slices of your aunt's homemade Thanksgiving pie, you might have said something more assertive like, "Aunt Molly, thank you so much for going to all the trouble. I've actually had some recent successes dealing with my body image and eating properly, so I'd love to have half a slice of your beautiful pie today ..." Or you can let her know how appreciative you are, that you are full at the moment, and you'd love to take a piece home with you to eat later.

This very same thing happened to me for years when I had to fly home for Thanksgiving every single year. It was horrible. I dreaded every single minute of it. It wasn't that my mother baked anything for me. But, they always bought my favorite pie: French Silk. I always felt obligated.

Finally, one year I told my brother *not* to buy it on my account. His response was, "We don't buy it for you. We all eat it, too." Man, that just sucked. I actually felt worse after he said that, but to tell you the truth, I was kind of relieved. From that day forward, I simply *chose* never to eat that pie again. (Well, for a few years anyway!)

And, you know what? No one even cared! They weren't watching my every move; the table wasn't waiting with bated breath to see what I'd eat, how much of it, and how big a slice. It was simply my *perception* that I felt obligated to begin with! (Can you believe how narcissistic I was being to think that it was *all about me* to begin with?) I spent all of those years dreading the Thanksgiving family reunion with all of that food, and for what? It was all in my very own twisted mind! Had I only spoken up, my appreciation and enjoyment of the holidays would have started much sooner. Actually, now I eat what I want (including the pie) because you know what? Food is not my enemy, and neither is my body!

All of those years, feeling obligated, without cause. Phew! No more. I chose to be assertive and, while my words might not have conveyed this sense of new-found assertion, my actions certainly did. And when it's a *choice* it feels awesome! No guilt, no bingeing, no purging, and no restricting! Ha! How does *that* feel, ED?

Trigger #5:
Environmental Cues

How does our environment shape us? What cues does it give us that affect our behaviors, actions, and speech? Thanks to our environment, we may end up doing things that we simply do not plan to do.

Have you ever been, or know someone who has been, in treatment for drugs or alcohol? If so, the one thing they tell the individual upon discharge is to stay away from the people, places, things, and situations that remind them of where they used to get high.

The reason is clear: they have associated those circumstances with the drug. This is more than mere coincidence, this is pure classical conditioning. Even if they do not ingest the drug, upon seeing or being around the people, places, things, or situations they associate with the drug (often quite strongly), their body physiologically gets the same feeling that they used to get when they *did* consume the drug.

That feeling is no longer merely emotional, but physical. Their bodies feel it as well as their brains. That's how strong the association has become. You may remember, way back in our very first official chapter together, how we talked about classical conditioning. I discussed how the soundtrack from *Jaws* conditioned audiences around the world to expect something violent, creepy, or gross? Our fifth emotional trigger, environmental cues, play a big part of all that.

How does this relate to your ED? Well, let me explain. Maybe you and your family used to travel to a very specific spot each summer for a family vacation. Let's say this place has very strong food memories for you, such as a Coney Island hot dog or Florida key lime pie or theme park snacks shaped like famous rodents or cartoon characters.

These vacations are irrevocably linked with childhood memories associated with food. The food equals comfort, fun, or happiness. What happens when you return to the favorite vacation spot as an adult? This environment may trigger such an intense emotional reaction that your instinct is to overindulge. At that point, your ED-inspired instincts to feel guilty and to seek power and control by restricting or binge-purging kick in.

How do you react? Well, if you've recovered and you've gained the coping skills you need, most likely you'll be able to use your tools and skills to offset any self-destructive behaviors that you may have reverted to in the past.

As you can see, triggers can be internal or external, controllable or uncontrollable. If, for instance, you already know that dealing with a specific person can trigger an ED behavior, you have three choices: (1) avoid that person, (2) engage in your ED behavior, or (3) plan ahead. The choice is yours. Just make sure you recognize the consequences ahead of time and prepare for them.

Unfortunately, at times there will be things that we cannot choose to avoid forever. Many times these may be our very own family members. And, of course, I am not recommending that you cut yourself off from them indefinitely, nor am I suggesting that you simply permit yourself to allow ED to take over.

So, then what? The choice is *still* yours. It's time to learn to plan ahead: to learn to cope and to deal with those circumstances in a more effective manner. If we have the fortune of knowing ahead of time that we will be facing an uncomfortable situation, we have to have a plan of attack. So my suggestion is that we prepare for the unforeseen circumstances now.

Defending yourself against triggers: a guide

The main thing I want you to remember is this: some triggers are unavoidable. Sorry; they just are. I can't prescribe a pill to blot them out or suggest a trigger-free zone where you can live, hermit-like, for the rest of your life.

Say it with me: "Some triggers are unavoidable." You can't shut yourself off from *people*, you have to go *places* and we all need, use, and experience *things*. Unfortunately, we will never be able to control such outside influences, even when so many of them happen to trigger unpleasant circumstances in our lives.

So what are we to do about them?

Preparing for triggers

Since we cannot eliminate triggers altogether, the next best thing is for me to help you prepare for when you inevitably come up against an emotional trigger. It is clear that triggers can be internal (you wake up every Monday with a feeling of dread) or external (you see a fast food restaurant on the corner), controllable (you can avoid your ED-inducing relatives by going away every Thanksgiving, but I'm sure your family won't be thrilled about this; uh oh, there's that obligatory feeling again, right?) or uncontrollable (you inadvertently run into an old friend on the street who reminds you of some of the worst times of your life).

With regard to triggers, such as a specific individual, that you already know can create an eating, binge/purge frenzy, or cycle of restriction while you are near that person, you have three choices:

1. Avoid that individual forever;

2. Engage in your ED cycle;

3. Plan ahead for this meeting.

Your personal triggers worksheet

Although we cannot control others' behaviors, we can certainly control how we choose to react/respond to them. For example, what if someone says to you, out of the blue, "You're fat." In this world where obesity, or anything even remotely close to it, is considered the last acceptable prejudice, it's entirely likely to happen at some point.

In such a classless situation, here are your choices:

1. Run away crying and binge and purge;

2. Starve yourself for three days;

3. Journal your thoughts and feelings;

4. Continue eating your healthy meal plan;

5. Over-exercise until you pass out.

My suggestion to you (yep, this is my famous homework time) is to write out a chart with all possible scenarios of things that may have happened to you, how you responded in the past, and how you can now respond in a more healthy manner. Then, when the circumstance arises next time, you'll be armed and ready for a much more effective and healthy way to cope!

This is the best way to get ED out of your life for once and for all!

Use the first column to record any circumstances that may have led to an unproductive, dysfunctional, or self-destructive response. Next, record your reaction to the situation as it occurred. Finally, in the third column, write a new and healthy reaction to prepare for a similar situation in the future. Preparation is your main tool for a healthy and productive lifestyle.

For example, let's fill in the first column using the following real-life scenario:

*   **Situation:** *My father told me I am fat.*

- **My Reaction:** *I went to my room and ate an entire bag of chips and a box of cookies. Then I purged.*

- **My New Response:** *Tell him how it makes me feel.*

See how you evolved from a negative reaction to a positive one? Relax; it takes time. Preparing for when we encounter triggers is a habit we must form. It doesn't happen overnight. Still, the more you use this worksheet (you may want to make copies for future use) the easier the habit will become. Remember, practice makes proficient!

SITUATION	MY REACTION	MY NEW RESPONSE

Letters to ED, to our bodies, to ourselves:

Dear Body,

I can't believe I'm actually going to make it to my twenty-fifth birthday in less than two weeks. I have used and abused you for eight and a half years now. Between the bingeing, purging, and starving I am amazed and baffled by the fact that you are still functioning and look healthy to everyone else.

How have you not shut down yet? I am lucky to be alive. I want to be alive. I am sorry for the way I have and continue to treat you. I do love you and am trying to get better. Thank you for being so strong and not giving up on me. We'll get through this. Let's think positive. Think how healthy and happy we used to be. I want that back, and I'm sure you do too.

"Rachel"

CHAPTER 8

Create Your Own Happy Ending!

"Everything you are against weakens you. Everything you are for empowers you."

—Dr. Wayne Dyer

Do you know what it feels like to be empowered?

I do.

I can say that now, openly, honestly: I know what it feels like to be empowered. That's why I became a therapist. That's why I wrote this book. That's why I sat down, every day, for over a year to make sure that every word on these pages moved forward in a logical, transformational, empowering way.

I have felt what it's like to live an empowered life. It may read easy, but it hasn't been easy for me to say. There were times when I felt so low I thought I'd never get out of bed. There were times when it felt better not to go on than to live the lie another single, solitary day. There were times when I thought I had no one else but ED; times when I thought no one but ED cared.

Now I know better. Now I know that the only person who has to care about me is *me*. That was the real secret to my transformation: I mattered. First. Foremost. Every day. I mattered. I came first. My thoughts were valid and important. I had something to say. I had a reason to live; a reason to go on.

Now it's your turn. This book has been about giving you power. More specifically, it's been about giving you back the power you already had. There was nothing really new in this book. The theories weren't mine, though the experiences were. And even those experiences weren't entirely unique; I'm sure at times they sounded downright familiar. All I've really done is put my passion to paper and my experience in the field of psychology to good use for a fight I believe in.

That's *you*, by the way! You are what I believe in most. The theories, the behaviors, the feelings, and the emotions are all tools to get to the heart of you. But I can't do it alone, nor can your family, your friends, or your therapist. You must believe in yourself. You must feel worth the fight. You have to believe that tomorrow will be better than today and that the day after will be even better than tomorrow.

But better tomorrow can't be enough. Every day must matter; every hour must count. Happy people aren't freaks or lucky or anomalies. There are millions of people out there, walking around right now, maybe even sitting beside you (or writing this book) who are genuinely, authentically, fantastically content. They are not geniuses or rich or famous or perhaps even extraordinary in any other way, except for the fact that they realize every day is a gift and refuse to waste another minute on useless self-talk, negative emotions, or years of emotional baggage.

In fact, they are just like you, with one minor difference. The only thing they've done differently than you is to choose a different path. Every morning they wake up and make a conscious choice to be happy. They may be overweight, underweight, ill, healthy, rich or poor. They may face work pressures that are incredible, debt that seems insurmountable, or family problems that are too depressing for words. But they realize intrinsically that those problems won't disappear simply because they are sad. Problems exist whether or not you worry them to death or choose to put them in proper perspective.

You have a choice: happy or sad, hopeful or gloom and doom. The choice you make now won't just affect this moment, or tomorrow, or the next day. The choice you make now gets piled onto every other choice you've ever made, day after day, year after year. You can't roll back time and undo those unhealthy choices, but you can start making better ones right now, today.

Personally, I made my own choice some time ago. You see, for many years my heart was guarded, blocked off, and solitary. From past hurts and betrayals (whether real or imagined), I had built a wall around my heart to keep out those who might do me harm. Over the years, as I grew away from harmful influences and drew closer to myself, the wall around my heart began to crumble. Cracks formed and fissures split and slowly, very slowly, I let the outer world back in.

As the wall came down, so did my inhibitions. It seemed right for me to live more openly, expressing myself more freely and responding to others as they expressed themselves to me. I saw the world differently; I felt the world differently. There was more good than bad; I was more happy than sad.

I can't take credit for breaking down the wall all alone. I had help—call it a creator, a source, a kindness—but an unseen force allowed my wall to crumble just when I needed it most. For in erecting a wall to keep away the outside world I had also closed my heart off from myself.

As my wall came down and my eyes opened, I could see, and create for myself, the world I wanted to live in. My hope is that someone or something helps tear down your wall. I know you've needed to protect yourself in the past; I know your wall has helped seal out the harm that exists in the world. But now the time has come for you to break down that wall and see again. Feel again.

Live again.

Love again …

When I loved myself enough, I quit settling for ED.

A word about change

Well, we finally made it! Welcome to our final chapter together, a chapter that hopefully finds you ready for change. This chapter is about change: my change, your change, and our change.

A note about my change: my change was my choice. It happened to me. I went through it, I lived it, I endured it, and I survived it. In many ways, it will sound similar to your change. In many ways, it will be different. What I want to point out is this: what I did belongs to me and what you do belongs to you.

I do not want to encourage, support, or endorse a particular way of hanging out with ED. So if you don't hear *how* I purged, or where or when or the down and dirty details, it's because I don't want you to know something more than you already do about doing something we both know you shouldn't. Kapish?!?

A note about your change: your change is uniquely your own. It will happen to you, on your timeline, and in your own space, place, and time. I share what happened to me because I hold it out as a beacon of hope, because it taught me so much, and because we learn best by experiencing insight, growth, and change for ourselves. I wish that I could take your journey for you, but only you can change you.

A note about our change: we have already changed. I thought I was healthy before, but writing this book has filled me with a new sense of hope and encouragement for the future. Revisiting my own process has helped me deal with so much: my family, my friends, my clients, and myself. It is my hope that by beginning our transformation together, we can both be stronger for it!

Now, for my change ...

How I survived ... lived ... soared!

Let's get one thing straight right now: survival is not the goal here. We survive to get somewhere else; we do not exist to survive. Even living has its limits. To truly experience life to the fullest we must not merely survive, not just live, but *soar!*

Still, we have to crawl before we walk, walk before we run, and run before we soar. And so I survived, as we all must do, the best I could. It wasn't pretty, it wasn't fun, and it damn near killed me, but as you can see, survive I did ...

How I survived

> *"Dark clouds may hang on me sometimes*
> *But I'll work it out ..."*

> —Dave Matthews Band, *Dancing Nancies*

My survival story isn't pretty. It's not hearts and flowers, I'll tell you that much. The details that follow are as messy as they get. At some point, you might even think I'm making them up; the events are so outrageous and seemingly unlivable. But at that point I will remind you what most nonfiction authors often say: "Truth really *is* stranger than fiction!"

As you will shortly see, my eating disorder pretty much consumed my entire conscious life starting from about age twelve when I put myself on my first "diet." Why wait around? I recall weighing my food on one of those Weight Watchers scales, all the way back then.

I wouldn't eat a morsel more or less than what *I had determined* was right or wrong for myself. I became addicted to food grams, calories, and the scale. The numbers were all that mattered. I am sure many of you who are reading this know exactly how this goes!

Below is a list of my survival statistics (what I merely went through to be among the living). It's not pretty, but it's mine:

- 1976. My friend commits suicide by a gun shot to his head. Open casket at funeral.

- 1984. (One week after turning twenty-one) I had a cystectomy; a tumor in my fallopian tube the size of large grapefruit would have exploded within twenty minutes and killed me had I not been rushed to the ER to have it removed. Its development was attributed to poor nutrition, restricting, bingeing, purging, drug and alcohol use and abuse, late nights, little sleep, the wrong crowd, etc. (Sound familiar yet?)

- 1985. (Age twenty-one; six months after cyst in fallopian tube.) Tumor on rectum and internal hemorrhoids all surgically removed. These were both attributed to overuse and abuse of laxatives.

- 1987. (Age twenty-three) Beat up by boyfriend. Broken cartilage in nose; complete devastation; turned to ED, of course. Who else would come to the rescue? Admitted myself to the hospital for suicide attempt; called Mom collect. Amazingly, when I told her where I was, she passed the phone right to Dad and said nothing to me.

- 1987. (Age twenty-four) Uncle Fred died of AIDS. My only pillar; my best friend; my life! Complete devastation. Then, I find out that in his delusional AIDS-infested mind on his death bed, he had mumbled some sad untruths to my grandmother about me, things that *still* hurt to this day. It exacerbated my love affair with ED for years to come.

- 1988. (Age twenty-five) I contracted viral meningitis, taking me out of work for two months to stay in a dark room drinking only fluids. The disease was attributed to unknown causes, but in my own knowing mind I attributed it to poor nutrition and poor overall healthcare from years of abuse to my body. Of course, ED never let me tell anyone about my love affair with him!

- 1989. (Age twenty-six) Rape, pregnancy, and abortion, all thanks to the low self-esteem that ED caused me. As usual, I was forced to survive through this trauma *alone*. Locked myself in apartment for a month—alone. Drank alcohol, smoked cigarettes, starved myself. Depression set in big time. No one to help—but ED.

- 1989-1991. More suicide attempts. ED to the rescue.

- 1994. (Age thirty) Marriage (against my better judgment and only due to social pressures of being an old maid) and compulsive overeating began in full swing, because my husband was controlling and abusive (physically, sexually, verbally, you name it; you'll read about all of that in my next book!). Well, why wouldn't he be abusive? He said I was fat and uglier than sin! No more restricting, it was too draining. No more purging, it was killing me. The food was my friend, right ED? Then it got bad! He beat me to near death, and, amazingly, my parents insisted I stay with him. I left with $58 in the bank!

Of course, these are just the highlights. There was so much more in between each life-altering, life-shattering event, but one day I'll get to spill it all in my autobiography. For now, as is so often the case, this is just the tip of the iceberg.

Why do I relay all of this? I don't want to depress you or give you TMI (Too Much Information) about my own life, but it's important to see how quickly life's devastations can add up. Day after day, year after year, we all face hurts that accumulate, like sedimentary rock, until at last our self-talk is so negative, our emotional baggage so heavy, our pre-programmed reactions so vulnerable, that it seems almost inevitable that we hook up with ED at some point.

My goal with this terrifying list of ingredients is to show you that into every life a little rain must fall—though sometimes it feels like a hurricane—but with proper choices, therapy, treatment, and, most of all, *knowledge*, we don't have to add insult to injury. We don't have to wind up in the arms of ED!

The difference between surviving and living: a starter kit

How did I finally decide to stop merely surviving and begin to live? It was no accident; it was a conscious decision. I couldn't just wake up one day and turn the "survive" button off and the "live" button on. I had to consciously switch my settings; I had to reprogram myself to change.

That's the good news: conscious decisions are entirely within our control. We don't have to wait for a bolt of lightning or a divine message or even a sign from above. It begins slowly, one day at a time, one decision at a time, one set-back at a time, one frustration at a time, and with a lot of perseverance, but not with time alone can we heal sufficiently.

We must use that time to act; we must take that time to grow. Below are the ways in which I personally chose to live rather than merely survive. May the lessons I learned help you save time along the path to healthfulness and walk it more closely with each passing day:

- **I chose to learn.** You have made the same choice. Learning is more than just sitting in a classroom taking notes. Reading is learning. Listening is learning. Observing yourself is learning. Making a change is learning. To truly understand yourself you must choose to learn about yourself, about your disease, about ED, about survivors, about your family, your friends, your emotions, and about all the things we've been talking about since page one of this book. The minute I began learning about what I had was the minute I started healing from it. Introspection is the key! It's tough; it's painful; it works!

- **I changed my self-talk.** My self-talk was devastating most of my life. It was so loud, so obnoxious, and so deadly to my self-confidence that I literally couldn't hear myself think anything but negative thoughts. Changing my self-talk was one of the very first ways in which I sought to take back control over my life. It wasn't easy for me; it won't be easy for you. But you *can* do it …

- **I changed my perception of me.** I was at the root of all my problems. Outside forces intruded—they had been for years—but only after I was able to change my own perception of myself was I able to deal with those outside forces healthfully. It all starts from the inside out!

- **I journaled every day; all day.** In so doing, I became more and more introspective … enduring the pain and appreciating it as well. By writing down my emotions and getting a grip on how I felt and what I felt, I could truly appreciate what I'd been through and actually enjoy where I was heading. Journaling helped me do everything on this list before it, and everything after it. It was my way of addressing every emotion I had; of validating it, and of choosing to respond to each one more positively.

- **Baby bye, bye, bye.** I said good-bye to bad advice, bad doctors, and bad people who really didn't understand or didn't care to understand. None of us live in a vacuum. I couldn't heal myself if I kept the same damaging people around, day after day.

- **I removed myself from unhealthy friends.** I use the term "friends" loosely, because unhealthy friends actually turn into something quite the opposite when you are trying to heal yourself. Quite often as we get better our "friends" try to drag us down, so by eliminating them you can continue your progress toward health. Do not feel guilty for cutting "friends" off. If they're real friends, they'll understand and they won't be the friends you'll need to cut off anyway. If they don't understand you and what you're trying to do for yourself, if they resent you and make you feel guilty, then they were never really friends to begin with. I said good-bye to some lethal friends and truly stayed alone for a good long time until I healed myself. When I felt better, I attracted healthier friends naturally.

- **I stopped listening to unhealthy family members.** Your family can be a great source of solace as you begin the healing process; they can also be a source of strain. There is no one we listen to like our families. When they are behind us and supporting us in a healthy manner, we need to listen. When they are downgrading us and making us feel bad for doing well, then we need to stop listening. We can't choose our family, but we can choose not to listen to them when what they are saying is damaging to us. Your therapist can help you decipher who's who and work with your family to educate them in how they can be most supportive!

- **I recognized that I knew myself better than anyone else knew me.** At first, everyone had their opinions about what was wrong with me. I was too fat, too tall, too short, too stupid, too average, too this, or too that. As I began doing all of the other things on this list, I realized that no one knew me as well as I knew myself. That immediately invalidated all of their opinions. I could no longer trust anybody but myself. That didn't mean I didn't let in others over time, but for awhile you must truly rely on yourself, your knowledge of yourself, and your vision for yourself.

- **I not only recognized that many others *really were* jealous of me, but I finally allowed myself to admit it, and realized that those same people gave me advice based on their motives and their projections.** There's nothing people hate more than seeing someone else succeed. In fact, in social psychology, there is a theory that purports, "misery loves miserable company." (How true is that?) Even those who profess their undying love for you will try to drag you down if you begin to raise yourself too high (if the other person is lacking in self-esteem him or herself). It's human nature, I suppose. But it's also human nature to choose. In this case, you must choose to listen to yourself, to trust yourself, and to belief in yourself. You must do this even when what others say isn't congruent with the way you feel.

- **I gained invaluable insight into others' motives, including family, friends, colleagues, even my very own therapists.** Betrayal is an ugly word; it's an even uglier habit. But betray you some people will, even those closest to you. Beware when negative language creeps into the mouths of those who should be supporting you, not downgrading you. Know that you are on the right path and that, no matter what your friends, family, and above all ED may tell you, only you can walk it to the end. Of course, this is not to imply that anyone is "out to get you" in any manner. Most people want to help; they just don't know how. I want to make it clear that people should be trusted, valued, and appreciated … unless or until they give you reasons to feel otherwise.

- **I vowed to trust my own intuition.** Your mind and your gut have belonged to ED so long it will be hard to reclaim at first, but in many situations during the healing process your mind and gut are all you have to rely on. Learn to trust your instincts. Believe me, your desire for self-protection is stronger than ED's desire for your self-destruction. You can beat him; you must trust yourself to do it.

- **I vowed to honor my body.** Your body is a precious, inviolate being. We have abused our bodies so long; we have done them a grave disservice. When you can once again see your body as a beautiful temple and treat it with respect, you are well on your way to stopping those behaviors that make ED so happy!

- **I learned to forgive all family members and those who hurt me.** Forgiveness may seem impossible at first, but it's absolutely imperative that you find it in your heart to forgive. While I could never entirely forget what happened with certain family members, I know now that they did their best, and now I am living for me, without blame displaced anywhere else! First and foremost, of course, we must always remember that the first reason to forgive is for us, not for the other person. Forgiveness lifts the weight of burden (and anger) off of our shoulders and provides the extra energy that we need to forge ahead; we can use that fuel for our recovery. If, over the course of time, wounds are healed and relationships strengthened and family bonds tightened, that is a wonderful side effect of forgiveness. But we must first apply the "cure" of forgiveness to ourselves.

ED was the question; love was the answer: *how I lived!*

"Love's the only house big enough for all the pain in the world …"

—Martina McBride, from *Love's the Only House*

Armed with my list of healing rights, I was finally able to love that person who I'd ignored for so long: myself. I could finally see what I'd been doing to myself, and it was a feeling that took some time getting used to. It's not easy to look ourselves in the mirror of reality and radiate health after it's been smudged and besmirched by lies and self-hate for so very, very long.

But once my eyes were opened to the truth, and nothing but the truth, my vision cleared with each passing day. I learned to love myself, the life I was leading, and the person I was becoming. Along the way I had to deal with my feelings for others. I learned that I had a love/hate relationship with many people in my life. These are just some of them:

I *loved* my grandmother. I wanted her to love me. Instead, I used ED … as a cushion to keep my grandmother's love. What I never realized is that she always loved me unconditionally anyway! I love my grandmother to this day! As much as her own perception had hurt me because of my own twisted, ED-infested mind, I have *learned* that it's me and not my grandmother that was the culprit. Sally is a wonderful grandmother and a kind woman and has been a pillar of strength that I admire. She's been my rock and my inspiration to soar to my greatest potential. She has always loved me and always will … no matter what my size, shape, or weight! Her hang-ups are hers, not mine!

I *loved* my mother. I wanted her to love me. Instead, I used ED … to help her love me, too. But I realized later that my mother wasn't capable of loving me, because she never had the bonding experience with her very own mother that a child requires in order to provide that to her own daughter. There was a void in my mother's world and she filled hers with food, just like me. Can you blame her? Sally was *her* mother. Sally starved Mom when she was a kid, always telling her how fat she was and pulling food away from her too. Even her very own father used to tease her, telling her that he'd have to weigh her on a freight scale. And the saddest part is that my mother wasn't even a heavy kid!

The only difference now is that *I* have chosen to forgive *my* mom and feed *my* body what's healthy, but Mom still rebels against *her* mother. *I've* chosen to learn, grow and move on; Mom still overeats and comforts herself daily with chocolate. Doesn't leave home without it, right Mom? Sorry for saying these things, Mom ... but I care about your health, and I love you. And I know now that you love me too.

Mom's hang-ups are hers, not mine!

I *loved* my uncle Fred. Yes, the one who made me gag on my own bile while pushing me to my physical limits in the gym! I wanted him to love me. I used ED ... to help Fred love me. What I never understood is that he loved me unconditionally all along. When I graduated from college in 1985, Fred wrote me a letter that said, "Susan, You have proved that one person can have both beauty and brains. Congratulations. Love Aman." (his stage name). I am holding this letter in my hand as I a write this. It means the world to me.

I miss him dearly and think of him daily! He may have sent me into the arms of ED earlier in my life, but I have forgiven him as well.

I grew up and learned that Fred, too, struggled with issues of self-esteem all his life. He had to live his life in secret because his own father ignored him and treated him like a second-class citizen. Fred used his own ED-filled mind to find his self-esteem through his body building and other various addictions. I know all of this now, and I have long forgiven my uncle. I only wish he were here to see me now. He'd really be proud of me, because, for once in my life, I'm healthy and truly at peace from the inside out! His hang-ups were his, not mine!

How I soared

> *Could I have been anyone other than me?*
> *Could I have been, oh, anyone other than me?*
> *Could I have been anyone?*

> —Dave Matthews Band, *Dancing Nancies*

As you can see, survival is not quite the same as living. When we are surviving, we are merely "getting by." We are functioning, sometimes solely on autopilot, struggling to exist in the most trying of times. But when we truly live, when we actually soar, it is more than merely surviving or "just getting by." It is living as God truly intended us to live.

My relationship with my family, as you can see, was one that often felt like "survival of the fittest." As I've aged and regained my health, I can now see things more clearly in perspective. Forgiveness comes with time, with maturity, and with a willingness to move on.

Moving on was key to my survival, to my living and, ultimately, to my soaring. I decided to take control of my own life. I decided to take control of my education, my beauty, and my health. I decided to recapture my sense of youthful enthusiasm, curiosity, and pride in myself. I had nothing to be ashamed of; I'd harmed no one. In fact, I'd done nothing wrong but listen to others rather than myself. I'd done nothing wrong but take far too long to begin my recovery ... and end my affair with ED.

I decided to say good-bye to many people along the way. Good-bye ED! Good-bye everyone who ever steered me in the wrong direction! I need no one who hurts me. I need no one who is out for their own motive. I only need *me* from now on! It's *me who matters most*, and that's it!

And, it's all of you who are friends with ED that matter the most! It's you who have the control to change your direction in life! And today's the day to start! Don't start tomorrow, not next week, not next year—today!

I don't want to soar alone.

I need some company.

Let's soar together ...

The business of you

Businesses are designed to make a profit. To earn a profit, most businesses invest a fair amount of time, money, and energy into something called "research and development." This basically just means testing new ideas and creating new products. It is how businesses are run; it is how businesses succeed.

What if you were to treat yourself like a business? What if you were to try and apply sound business principles to your own life? What if you looked at your health as a spreadsheet, and indulging in ED-like behaviors cost you dearly (as it so certainly does), and being healthy created a "healthy" profit? What if, instead of money, emotional health meant the same thing as emotional *wealth*?

Stay with me here; this concept is not so strange as it sounds. You, in effect, are your own business, and in order to grow as a human being it is vital to invest a certain amount of time and study and effort into that most valuable of all commodities: *yourself.*

One of the most important tools available, which will cost you nothing but a few moments of your day, is self-contemplation. Those quiet moments, given to inward searching to explore your feelings, thoughts, and reactions about various aspects of your life, constitute self-contemplation. It may not sound like a very active thing to do, but it can clearly impact your life in ways that are powerful, empowering, and uplifting.

Now, I want to suggest a very solid starting point for your new business plan. Each morning before getting out of bed (and while you are still relaxed from a good night's sleep) I want you to say, "I can handle, in a relaxed and easy way, any situation that arises today. The manner in which I respond is my decision. Others respond to me according to me; they respond according to my choice."

This is an attitude of empowerment; this is an attitude of control. Empowerment. Control. These are two principles that are missing from most people who deal with ED on a daily basis. They feel the opposite of empowered in the face of most situations; they feel powerless. They feel the opposite of control when faced with times of crisis; they feel out of control.

This attitude of empowerment and control can stay with you. It is all about being calm, being analytical, and being *in* control. Once you learn that ED is making you truly out of control, it's time to learn to reclaim *your* control! You do not have to be robot-like to be in control; you do not have to be asleep to be calm. Serenity and control can mean one and the same; there is strength and power in reacting calmly to situations that, in the past, have sent you spiraling into the arms of ED.

Take this attitude with you in all of your daily activities. You will be pleased and amazed at the responses to this new attitude when you see positive changes taking place. Within a very short period of time the anticipation of being able to handle stressful situations with ease will become an integral part of your life.

With the distractions from negative stress (realizing that some positive stressors can actually be good for us) now showing up in your "loss" column, your business venture will truly be on its way to success. Even with all you've accomplished, however, the "business of you" is still far from complete. It may be hard, but the only way to truly succeed is to "fire" ED once and for all!

What's next for you?

I have bittersweet feelings about ending our time together. On one hand I'm sad to see our time here end. On the other, I'm proud of you for hanging in there, and I realize that it shows in you a true resolve to change how you look at the past and how you face the future. I'm excited about what's next: what's next for me, and what's next for you.

In this chapter I've shown you how I survived, how I lived, and how I soared. It's not impossible; it's ultimately doable. I've laid it all out for you, from beginning to end. Some might say I've revealed a little too much of myself on these pages; others might argue I haven't revealed enough. I suppose my answer is that I tried to make it about *you*, but in the process I found it impossible not to share what I'd been through. I don't know how you approach a book about something so important, so significant, without leaving traces of you behind.

There's no way to walk through this jungle unaffected; everywhere you step there are wild animals waiting to tear you limb-from-limb. You must face the jungle wide-eyed and alert. We must keep a close lookout for the most dangerous predator of them all: ED. We must be ever-vigilant about where we go, what we say, how we think, and how we feel. I have talked at length about all of the above, and we now know that words are not mere letters formed together, but that emotions can be brought out into the light, discussed, assessed, and dealt with in such a way that the feelings we engage in and the words that we use can be healthy, positive, and uplifting.

What's next for you? Where will you be tomorrow, when there is no more of this book to read? What about next week, when my words have long since faded and my name becomes but a memory? What about next month, when the lessons I've taught have lost their meaning and the examples I used fused with your own?

What's next for you is up to you. I urge you to take your recovery seriously from this day forward. You are important, worthy, and beautiful. You are smart, engaged, and creative. You must believe that. You must believe in yourself in order to care for yourself. The one thing I see in all of my clients when I first visit with them is a disastrous sense of a loss of identity.

They are lost in their own skins, not knowing who they are or why anyone would care about them. They have talked themselves into feeling like such failures in the face of such a very cagey and serious disease that it is all they can do to lift their heads up and look me in the eye. Very often, they can't even do that. Only days, weeks, and sometimes months later can they take a good look at themselves. Only when they believe in themselves can they help themselves.

I don't know where you are in your recovery curve. At the very beginning, on the upswing, or on the downswing, racing toward good health and better days. Wherever you are, keep going. Wherever you've been, don't go back. You can only help yourself if you move forward. You can only move forward if you believe that a new you, a better you, a healthier you is waiting at the end of that recovery rainbow.

I'm here to tell you that you that you can achieve the life you've been dreaming of, if only you'll believe in yourself. Doctors like myself, books like this one, your family, your friends, your mentors, your coaches, and your teachers can only help you so much. The core, every day battle must be waged within; you must fight your own demons, and you must believe you can win … because you can! I did and I know you can too!

I am no one special. I am not an athlete, I am not an artist, I have no special talents, and I am an ordinary person, from an ordinary family, with an ordinary lifestyle. I worked hard despite a reading disability, took out college loans for all of my schooling, and did it on my own. You can too!

I am not writing this book because I am so different from you; I'm writing it because I'm *just like you*! The only difference is that I "woke up" (after years and years of hard work, dedication, defiance, and treatment) to discover that I was so much more than merely a victim of ED or a victim of my circumstances. That is my goal for you and my wish for you: that you discover how much you have going for you. You are more than a victim; you are even more than a survivor!

Now you just have to *start* surviving …

What's next? What's next is up to you. What's next is waiting for you, just around the corner, healthy and happy, safe and quiet, if only you'll peer in that direction and believe it can be so.

Write your own story

Well, that's my story. What about you? What does your story hold? A happy ending? A new beginning? Healthier activities? Or more of the same? Life with ED? Disasters around every corner? More sadness, more shame, more conflicting emotions and family affairs?

I know that too many ED stories end badly; I see those often as well. How often I've wished I could share with you the many (too many) calls from emergency rooms I get, night after night, where families cling to a loved one who is wasting away before their very eyes. But would that help?

This is a chapter about motivation; it is a chapter about healing. But you and I both know that recovery is a long and winding road; never forget that. This is not some bubble gum book about cute sayings and platitudes. I'm not peddling bumper sticker psychology. You and I both know this is deadly serious business, and I challenge you to write a happy ending for your own story.

You have the tools. It may be a starter set—the basics you'll need—but they are enough to keep you together while you seek the professional treatment I so desperately encourage you to solicit. The time has come to stand on your own two feet and face the world anew. I do not expect, nor do I recommend, that you hit the ground running. I know it will take many thousands of baby steps to walk the path set out before you.

A path to life's contentment is fraught with land mines. There will be people who don't want you to get healthy; one of them is ED. He will try to stop you at every turn. The harder you fight, the tougher ED fights back. You must stay strong and resist his wrath. Resist the urge to give up simply because you've gone too long without giving in. Disillusionment is a powerful ally to ED. It's so easy to see failure all around us; it's so easy to give up.

When you are tempted, remember to write your own ending. Don't merely rewrite the failures of the past, the endless nights of self-torture and self-abuse, and the keening and crying and starving, bingeing, and purging. Don't give in to those old behaviors as if there is no other choice.

You have a choice. If I've given you nothing else, I've given you that much. I have shown you that there is an entire profession out there just waiting to help you recover. I've shown you ways you can help yourself. What you have is a disease, not a curse. It can be reversed, it can be healed, and, best of all, it can be overcome.

Your story—your life—is just beginning. Whether you're eighteen or eighty you are starting a journey toward a more positive attitude and better health. It's not easy, but it's necessary. You must stay the course; your very survival depends upon it. How refreshing it must feel to face the first blank page of your life-long story; how scary it must feel to know that you must author every word on every page.

But you're not alone. You have family. You have friends, be they one or one hundred strong. You have coaches and mentors and neighbors and teachers and doctors and authors. We are here for you every day in every way we can be. Use us; utilize us. Visit my website (www.TransformEmpowerSoar.com) for a list of ED organizations worldwide, contact the National Eating Disorders Association (NEDA), come to my seminars, email me, contact your State Psychological Association for ED specialists in your area, I am here for you; I am available in a time of need. And that's just the beginning!

Enlist your support group and begin searching locally for a doctor to personally treat your case. Phone-in therapy can work in a pinch, but you need someone committed to you, near you, for weekly visits and one-on-one, personal counseling as well as group and family therapy.

Every book can be a beginning, but no book can be an island unto itself. Even the best fitness book suggests joining a gym or buying some equipment. A gourmet cookbook lists ingredients to purchase, to blend, and to savor. So, too, do I send you out into the world charged with a mission to find help where you are.

If you are reading this for someone else, I have listed on my website and in the Appendix to follow a variety of sources where you can find help. These databases and web links can guide you to local assistance wherever you live. There is help out there; now it is your time to find it.

Finally, continue writing your story. Never stop filling your pages with rich experiences, caring people, and lessons learned and remembered. The choice is up to you: Will you have a happy ending or a sad ending? Will your story be with or without ED? Will it be a story where you give into the temptation and revisit old behaviors, or one in which you emerge from the darkness where you've been living and survive to share the experiences with others as I have?

I think you know which ending I'm rooting for ...

Soaring outside the box

You will notice on my website, throughout this book, on my business card, and, most of all, in my personal philosophy the words, *Transform. Empower. Soar.* That's not just a slogan or a logo; but a process. That's the process it takes to overcome ED, to be rid of him for once and for all.

My personal and professional symbol (which you'll also see on my website, throughout this book, on my business cards and souvenirs, etc.) is a butterfly. Not just because I'm a girl or because "it's so pretty," but because I see the butterfly emerging from the cocoon of self-denial, self-distrust, and self-loathing that has been our lives for so long.

You and I, dear reader, have been in this cocoon long enough. Like a butterfly, it is time to break out of our cocoons and truly soar, flying high above all that has kept us pent up, sealed off, and shut out for so very long. Sadly, this cocoon is something we've built for ourselves. Even worse, once we're out of the cocoon of our own making, we still have one more obstacle to overcome thanks to our good friend ED.

ED is far more guileful than any cocoon of our own making. He traps us in a box, deep and dark, locking us off from everything we love and that makes us happy. ED locks us in that box and throws away the key. He shuts us away from our family, our friends, our hope, our happiness, and our very freedom to live life.

With the tools we acquire through empowerment, knowledge, treatment, discussion, networking, trust, and hope along our journey, we can finally pick the lock that ED has used to keep us down for so long. This book is not about living; it's about thriving. My words don't just urge you to survive; I want you to soar!

It's my time.

It's your time.

Please come soar with me …

Letters to ED, to our bodies, to ourselves:

Dear ED,

You came into my life and made it living hell,

"Look at your fat and disgusting body" at me you would yell.

Every time meals came around,

You would help me to be nowhere to be found.

We became best friends; two peas in a pod,

As I began to worship you like some almighty God.

When it seemed all of my friends were turning their backs on me,

You constantly showed up making me think "never alone will I be."

I felt so in control when we were together,

Letting my weight dwindle down to light as a feather.

"I can do anything I want now," I often thought;

But there was one thing I forgot.

How could I climb to the last rung on my ladder of dreams,

When all I had eaten in days were a few measly green beans.

The only support I had was from, you; Ed-Mr. Evil himself.

As I was the one who abandoned my friends shoving them to the back of the shelf.

You backed me into a corner and chained me down,

Even laughing at my emaciated body as it floated in the hospital gown.

"You're still not skinny enough, those doctors are all crazy"

You yelled "just get up off your butt and stop being so damn lazy!"

I became obsessed with exercising as much as possible and eating the least calories I could,

All the while hiding behind my sweatshirt and hood.

I started to go crazy inside,

As all I could do to everyone was lie.

When my darkest hour started to shine in upon me,

I felt something pulling on my arm, with no idea what it could be.

"I have nothing to lose but what's left on these already skin and bones" I came to realize,

But there you were; Ed, screaming, "you can still go down another pants size!"

Yet, for once, I took a leap of faith on my own,

Stepping out of my safety and comfort zone.

Much to my surprise I landed in a world filled with all shades of yellows,

And was greeted by the voices of many familiar fellows.

I immediately found numerous familiar faces in the crowd,

And back into their loving arms, me they allowed.

So now I have joined forces against you; you dirty little bastard!

And off of your hellish road I have diverged.

I no longer need your deceptive actions, words, and lies,

Nor will I be the one who cries.

I have united with some of your other so-called "friends,"

And our shattered lives we will start to mend.

Leaving you with the dust to kick up in your face,

Ed you have done nothing but fuck with me, you are a disgrace!

There is no room left in my future for you now,

Back into my life you, I will no longer allow.

My smiles are re-appearing and my laughs resounding all around,

As the old me has now been found.

So this is our final good-bye and farewell,

As I close your door that led to living hell.

Leaving you only in memories of the past,

Joining forces with those friends who will last.

So get out of my life, skedaddle, scram,

For you I no longer give a damn!

I'm now living my life for me; and only me,

Breaking away from these chains that once bound me to now run free.

I mark this as the time to move on without any kind of doubt,

Because thanks to my friends in recovery and Rascal Flatts I am devoted to being "running when the sand runs out ..."

Yours,

"Lizzie"

Resources, References and Recommendations

National Eating Disorders Association (NEDA)
(Formerly EDAP & AABA)
603 Stewart Street, Suite 803
Seattle, WA 98101-1264
Toll-Free (800) 931-2237
Phone (206) 382-3587
FAX (206) 829-8501

National Association of Anorexia Nervosa and Associated Disorders (ANAD)
Box 7
Highland Park, IL 60035
(847) 831-3438

International Association of
Eating Disorders Professionals Foundation
PO Box 1295
Pekin, IL 61555-1295
(800) 800-8126

Eating Disorders Anonymous (EDA)
18233 N. 16th Way
Phoenix, AZ 85022

Academy for Eating Disorders (AED)
6728 Old McLean Village Drive
McLean, VA 22101
(703) 556-9222

Eating Disorder Referral and Information Center
2923 Sandy Pointe, Suite 6
Del Mar, CA 92014-2052
858-481-1515

National Center for Overcoming Overeating
P.O. Box 1257
Old Chelsea Station
New York, NY 10113-0920
(212) 875-0442
Women's Campaign to End Body Hatred and Dieting

Alliance for Eating Disorders Awareness
PO Box 13155
North Palm Beach, FL 33408-3155
(561) 841-0900

Eating Disorders Coalition
609 10th Street NE, Suite #1
Washington, DC 20002
(202) 543-3842

Eating Disorder Council of Long Island (EDCLI)
50 Charles Lindbergh Blvd. Suite 400
Uniondale, NY 11553
(516) 229-2393

Harvard Eating Disorders Center (HEDC)
356 Boylston Street
Boston, MA 02118
1-888-236-1188

Massachusetts Eating Disorder Association, Inc. (MEDA)
92 Pearl Street
Newton, MA 02158
(617) 558-1881

Overeaters Anonymous
P.O. Box 44020
Rio Rancho, New Mexico 87124-4020
(505) 891-2664
FAX (505) 891-4320

The National Eating Disorder Information Centre (NEDIC)
CW 1-211, 200 Elizabeth Street
Toronto, Ontario
416-340-4156

Eating Disorders Association (UK)
First Floor, Wensum House
103 Prince of Wales Road
NORWICH, NR 1 1DW
Norfolk, UK
01603 621 414

Sylfiderne (The Sylphs)
c/o Elsebeth Sos Hansen,
Max Mullers Gade 11, 3.
DK-8000 Aarhus C
(+45) 40 60 59 54

The Eating Disorders Action Group
150 Bedford Highway, #2614
Halifax, NS B3M 3J5
(902) 443-9944

WINS
We Insist on Natural Shapes
PO Box 19938
Sacramento, CA 95819
1-800-600-WINS

ANAB Quebec
114 Donegani Boulevard
Pointe Claire, Quebec H9R 2V4
(514) 630-0907

Eating Disorders Association
Bryson House
38 Ormeau Road,
Belfast 7
IRELAND
Sackville Place,
44 Magdalen Street,
Norwich, Norfolk NR3 1JE.
Tel 080 232 234914

Center for the Study of Anorexia and Bulimia
(212) 595-3449
Administrator
1 West 91st Street
New York, NY 10024

British Columbia Eating Disorder Association
841 Fairfield Road
Victoria BC Canada
(250) 383-2755

Compulsive Eaters Anonymous—H.O.W.
PO BOX 4403
10016 Pioneer Blvd Suite 101
Santa Fe Springs, CA 90670
(310) 942-8161
FAX (310) 948-3721

Eating Disorders Professionals (IAEDP)
123 NW 13th St. #206
Boca Raton, FL 33432-1618
(800) 800-8126
FAX (310) 948-3721

Promoting Legislation & Education About Self-Esteem, Inc. (PLEASE)
91 S Main Street
West Hartford, CT 06107
(860) 521-2515

National Association to Advance Fat Acceptance, Inc. (NAAFA)
P.O. Box 188620
Sacramento, CA 95818
(800) 442-1214

Food Addicts Anonymous
(561) 967-3871

From the Therapist's Bookshelf: Recommended Reading

There is a preponderance of competitive titles that fall into one of the following categories: memoirs written by sufferers of eating disorders and therapists who specialize in eating disorders.

None of the titles listed below blend the two sub-genres, nor are they written by therapists who have themselves suffered from eating disorders. Regardless, the list below establishes a firm readership for books about eating disorders while revealing the "missing link" that *It's Not About the Weight* provides:

- *Life Without Ed: How One Woman Declared Independence from Her Eating Disorder and How You Can Too* by Jenni Schaefer (McGraw-Hill, 2003)

- *Feeding the Fame: Celebrities Tell Their Real-Life Stories of Eating Disorders and Recovery* by Gary Stromberg and Jane Merrill (Hazelden, 2006)

- *A Very Hungry Girl* by Jessica Weiner (Hay House, 2003)

- *Woman Redeemed* by Diana Kline (Authorhouse, 2005)

- *Reviving Ophelia* by Mary Bray Pipher (Muze,1995)

- *Dying to Be Thin: Understanding and Defeating Anorexia Nervosa and Bulimia—A Practical, Lifesaving Guide* by Ira M. Sacker (Warner Books, 1987)

- *Andrea's Voice: Silenced by Bulimia—Her Story and Her Mother's Journey Through Grief Toward Understanding* by Doris Smeltzer, Andrea Lynn Smeltzer, and Carolyn Costin (Gurze Books, 2006)

- *Surviving an Eating Disorder: Strategies for Families and Friends* by Michelle Siegel (Collins, 1997)

- *Wasted: A Memoir of Anorexia and Bulimia* by Marya Hornbacher (Harper Perennial, 1999)

- *Fat Girl: A True Story* by Judith Moore (Hudson Street Press, 2005)

- *Slim to None: A Journey Through the Wasteland of Anorexia Treatment* by Jennifer Hendricks (McGraw-Hill, 2003)

- *Life Inside the "Thin" Cage: A Personal Look into the Hidden World of the Chronic Dieter* by Constance Rhodes (Shaw, 2003)

- *Tales from The Scale* by Erin J. Shea (Polka Dot Press, 2005)

- *Bitter Ice: A Memoir of Love, Food, and Obsession* by Barbara Kent Lawrence (Rob Weisbach Books)

- *Beyond The Looking Glass: Daily Devotions for Overcoming Anorexia and Bulimia* by Remuda Ranch (Thomas Nelson)

- *Running On Empty: A Diary Of Anorexia and Recovery* by Carrie Arnold, Foreword by Susan Gottlieb, PhD (First Page Publications)

- *Your Dieting Daughter: Is She Dying for Attention?* By Carolyn Costin (Brunner/Mazel, INC.)

- *Losing It: False Hopes and Fat Profits In the Diet Industry* by Laura Fraser (Plume)

- *A Waist Is a Terrible Thing To Mind: A Wake Up Call* by Jan Phillips, Cathy Conheim, Christine Forester and a circle of women (Breakthrough Press)

- *Diary Of An Eating Disorder: A Mother and Daughter Share Their Healing Journey* by Chelsa Browning Smith, with comments from her mother, Beverly Runyon (Taylor Publishing Company)

- *The Weight Loss Diaries: A Tale of Binges, Guilt, Fat Days, New-me Shopping Sprees, Exercise, More Binges, and ... How I Learned To*

Deal With My Lifelong Weight-Loss Struggle by Courtney Rubin (McGraw-Hill)

- *The Starving Family: Caregiving Mothers and Fathers Share Their Eating Disorder Wisdom* by Cherly Dellasega, PhD (Champion Press, LTD)

- *Biting The Hand That Starves You: Inspiring Resistance To Anorexia/ Bulimia* by Richard Maisel, David Epston, Ali Borden (W. W. Norton & Company/Norton Books)

- *Insatiable: The Compelling Story of Four Teens, Food and its Power* by Eve Eliot (Health Communications, Inc.)

- *Ravenous: The Stirring Tale of Teen Love, Loss and Courage* by Eve Eliot (Health Communications, Inc.)

- *Perfect* by Natasha Friend (Milkweed Editions)

Please Keep In Mind

- EDs are *not about the weight*!

- EDs are *not about the food*!

- In the case of the emaciated anorexic patient, it *is* about the weight *first and foremost*. The individual *must* be medically stable before psychotherapeutic intervention can be most beneficial.

- Diet's *don't work*!

- What may start out as a simple vanity diet to lose of a couple of pounds may spiral into a severe addiction to ED.

- Diets may result in EDs or other disordered eating habits.

- ED thinking starts long before the first binge, purge, or restriction *behaviors* begin.

- EDs do not end when the behaviors cease. In other words, just because the behaviors stop *doesn't* mean the ED is gone!

- EDs are the thoughts, feelings, preoccupations, perceptions, ideas … not merely the behaviors.

- The behaviors are simply the manifestation of the underlying psychological problems.

- The underlying common denominators with ED sufferers are their perceived lack of control, hypersensitivity, and low self-esteem.

- EDs are about control, not about the weight or the food.

- Weight and food are merely the vehicles that the victim believes or says it's about.

- Weight and food are merely the vehicles that are used to express the victim's distress.

- Weight and food are the vehicles that are used as the victim's coping skills … until more effective skills are learned.

- Not everyone with an ED has been told *they* are fat or that *they* need to lose some weight.

- ED sufferers may merely overhear people make comments about other people such as, "They are getting heavy," or, "Man, she's putting on the weight" and begin to internalize those comments.

- People with EDs are highly sensitive individuals by *nature*. They deserve to be treated as such.

- There are a multitude of variables that precipitate the onset of an eating disorder. Let's not worry about whose to blame; let's take care of how to manage the illness today and move forward.

- Admitting an ED patient to the hospital merely for weight gain will *not* cure the eating disorder. The eating disordered preoccupations will still remain until proper treatment is rendered.

- Eating disorders are serious health conditions that can be both physically and emotionally destructive.

- People with eating disorders need to seek professional help.

- Early diagnosis and intervention significantly enhances the rates of recovery.

- If not identified or treated in their early stages, eating disorders can become chronic, debilitating, and even life-threatening conditions.

- There is no template for the treatment of EDs. Each patient must be cared for with an individualized treatment plan according to his or her unique circumstances.

- Eating disorders are *not* a choice. They are serious and potentially life-threatening illnesses which require a multi-faceted approach to treatment.

About the Author

Dr. Susan Mendelsohn

"Maybe if my mother didn't drag me off to weight loss clinics left and right as a child … and maybe if my daddy didn't tell me how fat or chunky I was … maybe if they made me feel like more of a person and less of a body."

—Anonymous ED sufferer

Dr. Susan Mendelsohn writes and consults for eDiets.com, Inc. Her columns reach millions of subscribers daily. Her support group and live lectures have drawn in hundreds of thousands of individuals seeking her professional insight.

"Dr. Susie," as she is affectionately known by her loyal clients, is a clinical psychologist professionally licensed in Ohio. She was a professor of professional psychology for fourteen years, resigning as an associate professor in 2003 before relocating to Cincinnati, Ohio to be closer to family.

Dr. Mendelsohn was honored by the *Cambridge Who's Who of Executives and Professionals* in 2006 as a Lifetime Member for achievements in her field.

Thanks to her engaging personality, Dr. Mendelsohn has been featured on radio and television and in various national magazines including *Low Carb Woman, Glamour, First for Women, The Daily Mirror* (UK), *The Business Courier, The Cincinnati Enquirer, The Cincinnati Post, Hyde Park Living, Cincy Jew-*

ish Living, Style and Leisure, The Wall Street Journal, WORK-TV-13 (Rochester, NY), WVXU, WXIX, NKY Magazine, WCPO, WMUB, WBOB talk radio, AOL, and many others.

Dr. Susie's workbook, *Why Weight?* guides the reader toward a lifestyle of overall balance and is not intended as a weight loss book. Written primarily to address the frequent questions posed to her by eDiets.com members, *Why Weight?* has provided solutions, answers, and a healthier approach to weight loss for its thousands of readers to date.

In addition to consulting for eDiets.com, Dr. Susie specializes in eating disorders and their related, co-morbid mental illnesses. Her areas of expertise are eating disorders, disordered eating, body image, relationship counseling, and stress management. She also has extensive experience working with those individuals who suffer from depression, anxiety, addiction, and physical, emotional, and sexual abuse—all in relation to her groundbreaking work helping sufferers of ED from the inside-out.

Dr. Susie follows a five-pronged approach in guiding her clients toward a successful future of inner peace, no matter what challenges they may be experiencing. In this five-pronged approach individuals must:

1. Identify their need to change;

2. Have the desire to change;

3. Gain the knowledge and tools required to change;

4. Have the belief in their ability to change (self-efficacy);

5. Implement or apply such change.

The naked truth of our being emanates from the inside out. Dr. Susie, clinical psychologist, possesses the skills, compassion, and experience to provide her clients with what it takes to learn to live life rather than merely survive it.

The butterfly logo on her website at www.TransformEmpowerSoar.com symbolizes the metamorphosis of how individuals journey through their lives in gradual, step-by-step fashion in order to make lasting changes for a lifestyle of mental, emotional, physical, and psychological well-being.

Just as a cocoon unfolds and undergoes metamorphosis, so does each human. We cannot simply pry open that cocoon and expect a butterfly to appear. If we attempt to do so, it will die prematurely. Humans must make gradual, healthy changes, just as a cocoon turns into a lovely butterfly in its due time.

Through her private practice, public lectures, and now *It's Not About the Weight*, Dr. Susie provides the tools and resources to assist her patients to transform their lives by empowering them to soar to their greatest potentials.

Every individual Dr. Susie works with is unique; each is in his or her own psychological space at any given moment and can be neither pushed nor rushed into growth or change.

There is no one right way to promote change. Each person is an individual and has their unique quirks when it comes to ED. Dr. Susie helps them within their own emotional, cognitive, and psychological frame of reference and potentials/abilities.

No matter what their challenges, Dr. Susie's patients are provided with unconditional positive regard and utmost respect. She also collaborates with other experts, providing a multi-faceted treatment approach for each of her patients.

Dr. Susie is a member of the American Psychological Association (APA), the National Eating Disorders Association (NEDA), and the Ohio Psychological Association (OPA).

978-0-595-41883-1
0-595-41883-X

Printed in the United States
98655LV00004B/30/A

9 780595 418831